DONALD TINDER

D0285793

EXISTENTIALISM
and
CHRISTIAN BELIEF

MILTON D. HUNNEX

Library of
New College Berkeley

MOODY PRESS ● CHICAGO

Copyright © 1969 by

The Moody Bible Institute
of Chicago

Acknowledgment is made for permission to quote from:

John A. T. Robinson, *The New Reformation?* Published in the U.S.A. by The Westminster Press, 1965. Copyright SCM Press Ltd., 1965. Used by permission.

David E. Jenkins, *Guide to the Debate About God.* Published by The Westminster Press. Copyright D. E. Jenkins, 1966. Used by permission.

John L. Austin, "Truth," from *Philosophical Papers.* Published by The Clarendon Press, Oxford, England. Used by permission.

Eric L. Mascall, *The Secularization of Christianity.* Published by Holt, Rinehart and Winston, Inc. Copyright E. L. Mascall, 1965. Used by permission.

Printed in the United States of America

Contents

Preface

This book constitutes a reorganization of ideas and material originally presented as a series of public lectures during the spring of 1967 at Western Baptist Seminary in Portland, Oregon, and in articles appearing in *Christianity Today* during 1965, 1966 and 1967. Chapter 2, "Honest to God or Honest to Man?" is largely an extensive revision and expansion of the article "A Theological Fifth Column?" which appeared in *Christianity Today*, March 26, 1965. Chapter 3, "Existentialism or Supernaturalism?" is also largely an extensive revision and expansion of the article "Have the Secularists Ambushed God?" published in *Christianity Today*, October 13, 1967. Chapter 7, "Is There a Religionless Christianity?" is a revision and expansion of the article "Religionless Christianity: Is It a New Form of Gnosticism?" which was printed in *Christianity Today*, January 7, 1966. Finally chapter 8 is an extensive revision and expansion of the article "Has the Spirit of Confusion Bewitched the Secular Theologians?" which appeared in *Christianity Today*, December 23, 1966. I am grateful to *Christianity Today* for permission to make extensive use of these previously published articles. Appreciation is also extended to Dr. Earl Radmacher, President of Western Baptist Seminary, whose interest in getting my seminary lecture series published was largely responsible for the publication of this book.

The essays that comprise this book are essentially philosophical. They attempt to argue the case for evangelical Christianity on rational grounds already familiar to philosophers and many liberal Christians. The reader will note that biblical references are few and far between, and no attempt is made to build a case on them. This will seem strange to those who are accustomed to biblical support for biblical Chrisitanity. The strategy is deliberate. Believers already know the case for evangelical Christianity as it derives from Scripture. Without the Bible, evangelicalism would have little to say. Evangelicalism takes a high view of Scripture and shows this by its affection and respect for it as the Word of God. Non-Evangelicals do not show or share their affection or respect in the same way as Evangelicals. Any direct appeal to the authority of Scripture would likely fall on deaf ears or get reinterpreted or explained away. Hence "the Bible says" approach is not my approach.

My thesis is that liberal Christianity is in trouble. It is in trouble not only because it has abandoned Scripture and orthodoxy but because it is shaky on its own grounds. If liberal Christianity is to make its case on certain rational and moral grounds, then it must be prepared to be judged on these same grounds unless, of course, it must finally appeal to sentiment alone.

I should not be taken as saying that evangelical belief is not in difficulty in trying to justify itself on rational grounds. I should be taken as saying that evangelical belief does not possess a monopoly of these difficulties as liberals often seem to assume. And I am saying more. I am saying that liberal Christianity is bankrupt in many ways and that Christians would do well to reconsider trading in the old model for a new model that may turn out to be a philosophical as well as spiritual lemon.

Harry Emerson Fosdick once noted that it was not a question of a new or an old theology but a question of a new theology or none at all. On the contrary I shall contend that it is not a question of a new or an old theology but a question of the same gospel or no gospel at all.

6

1

A New Reformation or a New Religion?

WHEN BISHOP JOHN A. T. ROBINSON published his book *Honest to God* in 1963 it soon became the popular symbol of the revolt against traditional Christianity. Professional theologians had already developed and promoted this revolt, but it was Robinson's little book that appealed to lay readers by the thousands. It popularized the "new theology."

Two years later the bishop published another little book called *The New Reformation?* In this book he expressed surprise at the stir over *Honest to God* and compared his own reflections on the stir with those of Luther's written a year after his famous ninety-five theses in which he says: "It is a mystery to me how my theses . . . were so spread to so many places."[1]

Actually neither author presented extensive arguments, but they triggered powerful forces. Luther was inviting a discussion of certain neglected or badly obscured biblical truths. The revolt against Rome that followed was no part of his original intention. Similarly Robinson raised the question Is there "a new mutation in Christianity?" Originally he intended, he says, merely "to draw attention to the contribution of Die-

---

[1]Luther, as cited in John A. T. Robinson, *The New Reformation?* p. 11.

trich Bonhoeffer," who—he notes later—has become "the John the Baptist of the New Reformation."[2]

For the past century and a half the ideas of thinkers like Feuerbach and Schleiermacher have been incubating in the minds of Western liberal theologians. Robinson merely brings to the surface the efforts of these theologians during this period to make the Christian faith more plausible and palatable to the modern mind. In one significant sense we could say that Robinson revives the efforts of the sixteenth century Reformers to bring Christianity to the people, but in another and very crucial sense, we must say that he rejects their Christianity and gives us instead a reformation of an altogether different kind.

The new Christianity that Robinson advocates is to replace the old Christianity. It does not resemble it in those features that matter the most. "The God of the Augustinian-Reformed tradition . . . is not only far from us, he has departed from us," writes William Hamilton.[3]

No Christian can afford to ignore the crisis in Christian belief today. "Without doubt we are in the midst of a vast new Reformation," Torrance reluctantly writes.[4] "What right have we to talk like this?" Robinson asks. "A convulsion such as shook Europe in the sixteenth century is not something we can expect every year, nor every century. . . . Nevertheless there is just such talk," he observes.[5] The Christian can no longer carry on as though nothing were happening or as though the whole idea were the wishful thinking of theological leftists. It is not, but there can be no doubt that they speak only for certain segments of the household of faith and not for the millions of believers all over the world. For believers the new existential theology rewrites the historic faith. For them it is evident that what is happening is not a

[2] *Ibid.*, p. 23.
[3] William Hamilton, as cited in *ibid.*, p. 14.
[4] Thomas F. Torrance, as cited in *ibid.*, p. 11.
[5] *Ibid.*, p. 10.

continuation of what Luther and the Reformers sparked in the sixteenth century but something alarmingly different. "What we are being offered," Mascall concludes in his *The Secularization of Christianity*, "is not a reinterpretation of the Christian religion but a substitute for it."[6] No segment of Christianity has escaped the impact of the new theology. Roman Catholic Leslie Dewart's *The Future of Belief* argues that not only does Christian truth change, but it *must* change. Even God must change. One Catholic reviewer lamented, "Dewart wants new truths and new doctrines, and he wants them at the expense of the old ones."[7]

What is developing before our eyes today could be finally more significant than the revolt in the sixteenth century. That revolt sought to restore New Testament Christianity on its own terms. The revolt today seeks instead to restate Christianity in nonsupernatural, secular terms. It is a revolt against the God of authority and the Bible, against the God of traditional Christianity. "That God must *die*," Robinson writes, "if man is to *live*."[8] He is "intellectually superfluous, emotionally dispensable, and morally intolerable."[9] The new Christian looks to a *post*-Christian faith for the future based on existentialism and universalism as the basic philosophical moods. Christian belief has no part of it. Christian belief is an anachronism. It must be abandoned together with the rest of the past, Robinson contends.

Compare this revolt with Luther's. Luther was entirely orthodox although not in the same way as some of his followers. It mattered greatly to him whether someone compromised God's authority or misinterpreted His Word. He was intolerant of many ideas. For him, faith had to rest on Scripture or it had no

[6] Eric L. Mascall, *The Secularization of Christianity*, p. 282.

[7] Frederick D. Wilhelmsen, *The Future of Belief Debate*, Gregory Baum, ed., p. 52.

[8] Robinson, p. 112.

[9] *Ibid.*, p. 107.

foundation. Truth was revealed in Scripture. It was not experimental, and it certainly did not change.

Today's "new reformation" is profoundly different. It sees universalism and abandonment of orthodox belief as the mark of its faith. "I welcome ... the sympathy with which much that I said in *Honest to God* has been received by many within the Hindu and Buddhist traditions," Robinson writes.[10]

Today's "reformation" is preoccupied with social issues. It wholly accommodates itself to what it believes to be the best insights of modern scientifically oriented men. It no longer seeks the Spirit's illumination of Scripture but finds Spirit to be a special quality of the common life. It rejects Scripture—to say nothing of the authority of Scripture. God is a special feature of *human* existence. He is an openness to the future of human community, the new reformers say. He is not the transcendent and sovereign Creator of heaven and earth. Personal regeneration does not identify the Christian. He is the "gracious neighbor" who identifies with the community of which he is a part. Specific beliefs have no part of the Christian way of life. The term "believer" is an inappropriate anachronism. Neither Scripture nor tradition provides norms for belief or action. Rather modernity is taken seriously as the norm by which all questions of Christian faith or human existence are settled.

This "new Christianity" is the reality which all Christians must face today. Perhaps to speak of it as a "new religion" would be misleading since it sees itself as religionless, as wholly secular. But is it a new reformation? It argues that believers fail to see that the familiar faith of the past is gone. It reminds believers that philosophers and poets have been telling them this for a long time. Nietzsche announced the death of God in the last century. And Christians are finally seeing and admitting it, we are told. This is claimed to be a universal experience. It is a matter of

10 *Ibid.*, p. 13.

10

being "honest to God." What's more, the "modernity" that believers rejected was, after all, what the Christian faith is really all about. Christianity is this-worldly rather than otherworldly. It is about man—not God.

But believing Christians rightly suspect that something is wrong. *Gott ist Anders* (God is different) is the German title of Robinson's *Honest to God*. It is also what believers find to be the case. The new gospel is no longer the familiar gospel of the New Testament. Robinson tells of a "friend . . . [who] found that he was able to take as many copies as he liked to East Germany [because] they thought it was atheistic propaganda!"[11] To whom is *this* gospel familiar? And for whom is it radical?

Since the publication of Robinson's *Honest to God*, the public has been confronted with a tide of "new theologies." There seems to be no limit to the boldness or novelty of the new "Christians." Each generation of speculative thought tries to outdo its predecessor, and the older generation looks on approvingly as though surprised but nonetheless pleased at the stir they started.

But despite the intellectual euphoria that seems to hold, all is not well. Bishop Robinson in his recent book, *Exploration into God,* has some second thoughts about Bultmann's "undue historical scepticism," his dangerous reliance on Heidegger's existentialism, and Van Buren's departure from "what was intended by classical Christian theology." Yet he still seeks to satisfy everyone with a kind of nontheistic personalism that seems to say that God is not a supernatural personal Being but a personal response to all of life, that is, a response to all there is *as if* it *were* personal. How this is to satisfy believer and nonbeliever is not at all clear. Yet this is, I believe, what the bishop is trying to do.

Robinson persists in following Tillich in holding with the new theology generally that faith depends as

[11] *Ibid.,* p. 106.

11

much on *disbelief* as upon belief. In 1964 he lectured at the opening of an Exhibition on Atheism, Eastern and Western, at the University of Frankfurt. His lecture was entitled "Can a Truly Contemporary Person *Not* Be an Atheist?" and he concluded that in an important sense he cannot. "For many people today," he said, "the only Christian faith which can be valid *for them* is one that takes over *post mortem dei,* after the death of God as 'God' has traditionally been understood." Hence we must acknowledge, he says, that "there *is* an important sense in which a person [who] is fully a man of our times *must* ... be an atheist before he can be a Christian."[12]

But does the bishop mean that some idolatrous god must die? If so, believers are with him. Or does he mean the traditional God of biblical theism, the God of Abraham, Isaac and Jacob, and the God of the sixteenth century Reformers, to say nothing of the God to whom Jesus referred as Father? This is not altogether clear in Robinson. It *is* clear, however, that other radical theologians like Dewart or Altizer mean precisely the latter God, and this is also precisely the sense in which Robinson's atheistic audience would understand him.

Yet elsewhere he insists that he has "not the least desire to weaken or deny the distinctive affirmations of the Christian faith." Among these he says he would certainly wish to assert "the centrality of the confession 'Jesus is Lord', in the full New Testament sense that 'in him all things cohere' (Col. 1:17) and 'in him the whole fulness of the deity dwells bodily' (Col. 2:9)."[13] But when he says "in the full New Testament sense" he means in *his* own existential nonpropositional sense, and that is not the "full New Testament sense" at all. The New Testament writers simply cannot be made over into contemporary existentialists even by an otherwise distinguished New Testament

---

[12] *Ibid.,* pp. 106, 112.
[13] *Ibid.,* p. 13.

scholar like Robinson. The fact is that the new theologians generally have so greatly altered the meaning of New Testament Christian language as to make it no longer recognizably Christian to believers. No doubt the new formulations make sense to some, but surely one would think that it is the inside active participant of the faith and not the outsider who speaks for the faith.

The new reformation wants to have something for everyone. Identify what it is that you think is Christian and what it is that speaks to your condition, and some theologian—perhaps the very same one—will find a way to meet your need and everyone else's too. There is, Professor Mascall correctly observes, "a very perplexing tendency among writers such as these to retain the word 'Christianity' while applying it to something that nobody would normally describe as Christianity and then to say that this new thing is *real* Christianity' or *authentic* Christianity' or 'the essence of Christianity' or 'what Christianity *really* is.' "[14]

Historically theologians have almost always borrowed the methods and models of philosophy to help them in their work. While this is to a certain extent necessary, it has also subjected Christian faith to the influence and the fate of that philosophy. When the philosophy in question is abandoned, the theology that leaned on it is threatened if not abandoned too.

Platonism in its many forms was the first philosophy of the Christian theologians, but its dualism and otherworldliness gave way to the more monistic and naturalistic philosophy of Aristotle in the thirteenth century. It was partly the distortions of biblical Christianity introduced by Aristotelian philosophy that prompted the Reformers to revolt in the sixteenth century. Unable to assimilate either the naturalism of Aristotle or that of the scientific revolution, Protestant theology eventually turned to idealism as the modern

14 Mascall, p. 6.

philosophy best adapted to Christian belief. Modern liberalism made its home among the idealists during the nineteenth century. After World War I it became apparent that idealism was ill suited to the twentieth century, and theologians as well as philosophers abandoned it. They turned instead to existentialism as the kind of philosophy that did appear to fit the mood and needs of the twentieth century. Existentialism seemed to be the best philosophy for getting at the problems of men caught up in swift-moving change.

Kierkegaard's powerful and astringent thinking was discovered and found full force in Barth's theology. Kierkegaard's existentialism had the advantage of being openly Christian. Everyone dipped into the new philosophical fountain for ideas. Men like Buber and Heidegger—neither of whom is Christian—provided the up-to-date philosophical inspiration. Existentialism established itself as the philosophy of the new theology and also endowed it with many of its own philosophical difficulties. For one thing, it is not particularly congenial to the logical and scientific mind upon which so much of contemporary culture depends. The alliance between existentialism and the naturalism of the space age is not an easy one.

The language of existentialism is obscure. It is largely symbolic rather than conceptual. Its interests and forms of expression are more nearly that of the poet than that of the precision-minded scientist. Moreover it is not at all clear what the existentialists are trying to say since they say so many things and do not by any means represent a unified point of view even within their own individual writings.

Actually existentialism is not a philosophy in the sense that Platonism or modern idealism is a philosophy. It is rather a general point of view that, despite its disunity, stresses certain things. It stresses human freedom not just to choose rightly but to create a subjectively meaningful world. It rejects attempts to discover general truth about man or his world. While most of us can find a great deal of good and meaning

14

in our world despite our fallen condition or the discouraging state of the world itself, the existentialist finds only chaos and nothingness. Man has nothing going for him but his freedom.

"Existence precedes essence," Sartre says. By this he means that there is no settled-upon purpose or meaning for human life. Everyone must take upon himself the responsibility to create himself and his world. Man is what he makes of himself—the sum total of his choices and acts—Sartre says. Aside from freedom there is nothing. Thus men must choose the truth in which they stand. They do not find it. It isn't given. "How am I to *become* a Christian?" Kierkegaard asks —not what does it mean to be one.

Unlike other philosophies, existentialism takes very seriously the fact and threat of death expressed in the wider ontological sense of nonbeing or nothingness. How we can come to terms with this threat is the overriding concern of the existentialist. Perhaps the best introduction to the existentialist manner and mood of thinking is Tolstoy's short story "The Death of Ivan Ilych."

No one can share the penetrating insights of Tolstoy in this short story and fail to see the close connection between the concerns of the existentialist and the Christian faith. No philosophy has, perhaps, so dramatically identified the human situation and the relevance of the Christian gospel as has existentialism. Yet despite—or perhaps because of—this, existentialism rewrites the good news of the gospel. It turns it into a *subjective* drama that overshadows and replaces the *objective* biblical drama of God, history and human salvation. It severs man from any objective supernatural support.

In existentialism—even Christian existentialism— God has to go because He is of all things the greatest threat to human freedom and responsibility. His judgment fills the prospect of death with dread. His world is per se absurd. He has been found out, so to speak, as the irrational restriction upon our present and fu-

15

ture. He must die, we are told, so that we can rediscover Him in the future of humanity itself or in some
form that is not the sovereign supernatural form of
the past.

Like some of the heresies of the early church,
Christian existentialism pits the new and good "god"
of Christian brotherliness and openness against the
authoritarian God of the Bible. Instead of praise and
gratitude for the gift of life and for divine creation
generally, the existentialist calls for the courage to be
ourselves in spite of the meaninglessness of things as
they are. Instead of eternal life in its full supernatural
sense he offers openness to others. This is the final
meaning of our lives. Jesus is the "*man* for others"—
not the Lord of creation and salvation.

Despite some of its apparent advantages as a philosophical prop for Christian faith, existentialism tends
to distort that faith. It has led to a reinterpretation
rather than a restoration of New Testament Christianity. It justifies atheism and finally edges out Christian
belief altogether very much like the proverbial camel
in the tent.

The contemporary theologian lacks the wisdom of
his counterpart of the sixteenth century Reformation.
He is too eager to make Christianity relevant by compromise and accommodation. The sixteenth century
Reformers made mistakes too. They were intolerant
and often blind to the cultural currents of their day.
But they were not Gnostics. They did not seek philosophical substitutes for biblical truth. They did not rest
their case on philosophical grounds. They saw what
the contemporary theologian fails to see: New Testament Christianity must stand on the New Testament
or it does not stand at all. They were not against
learning, but against compromise and accommodation.
They sought to reform the faith, not to replace it with
something new and different. This is why the current
revolt is not a new reformation. It is something else,
perhaps a new religion.

The new theologians are by no means agreed as to

what Christian truth is today. Bultmann and Macquarrie, for example, want to preserve the "essence" of Christianity, the *kerygma*, and believe that existentialism makes this possible. They would see the revolt as bad only if it led to the abandonment of the Christian *kerygma*. But the *kerygma* is not being abandoned, they argue. It is being recast in more viable form. Bultmann, for example, does not mean by "modern world view" the view that modern secular man is self-sufficient. He means the *scientific world view*. But other radical theologians mean both. Man come of age with a scientific world view is *both self-sufficient as well as scientific* in his view of the world, they argue. He simply does not need God anymore. Christianity as it has been known in the past is finished.

Thomas Altizer and Leslie Dewart, for example, welcome the "new Christianity" as something *genuinely new*. They do not say, as does Macquarrie, for example, that the gospel can be preserved through it all. Indeed it should not be preserved, even if it could be, they argue. That would be unchristian, they believe. They are not at all interested in resolving Bultmann's, Bonhoeffer's or Tillich's hermeneutical problems but in proclaiming a *new* gospel for a *new* age. Not only is the old Christianity no longer relevant, it must be abandoned by the Christian if he is to remain Christian. "Once we truly come to understand the Christian God as a ... dialectical process," Altizer writes, "we shall finally be purged of the Christian religious belief in the existence of a unique and absolutely autonomous God."[15]

I agree with radicals like Altizer or Dewart that there is indeed something radically different emerging today, but I do not, like them, see it to be the epiphany of God even though it no doubt has a place in God's scheme of things. I do not agree with the mediating positions which hold that the new theology is not an abandonment of the faith once delivered or

15 Thomas J. J. Altizer, *The Gospel of Christian Atheism*, p. 89.

17

that the hermeneutical problems can be resolved and the continuity of the faith preserved. I do not believe this can be done because of the inherent incompatibility of existentialism and a historic Christianity based on the authority of Scripture. Existentialists say that Christianity has a mission, not a message—to use Dewart's words. Their alternative proposals are largely philosophical derivations that are neither necessary nor desirable in fulfilling the Great Commission. Their mission is not that of the apostles. They lead to Altizer and not to the restoration of New Testament faith. Moreover they do not see themselves as reformers in the sixteenth century sense of the term. They see themselves as prophets of a post-Christian era. Robinson's phrase "the new reformation" is simply misleading if not downright wrong.

The purpose of this book is to examine some of the difficulties of the new existential Christianity and to show how it is a departure from New Testament Christianity. The subject is enormously complex partly because of the many issues involved and their highly technical nature but also because the new theologies are themselves unified only in their rejection of orthodoxy and supernaturalism.

I do not want to suggest that no good has come or can come of existentialism as an approach to Christian belief. But my task is not to create sympathy or appreciative understanding of existential Christianity. Rather it is to provide a philosophical critique of it on behalf of evangelical orthodoxy. Hence no attempt is made to be irenic. The new "Christian" is forthright in his rejection of orthodoxy. I shall try to be forthright in my answer to him. And while I hold for the authority of Scripture as the norm for Christian belief and practice, I do not invoke this authority in support of what I say. I instead appeal to what believers already know and to their sense of logical propriety.

I have nothing new in the way of philosophical speculation about Christian belief. I mean only to call attention to certain features of the arguments of existential Christianity that reveal their inadequacy either as refutations of orthodoxy or as proofs of new theological truth. For me it is Scripture and Scripture alone that defines what Christianity is all about. I suppose this is so because it is the New Testament paradigms that define my own experience and understanding rather than the paradigms of the romanticist writers of the nineteenth century or the radical theologians of today. Perhaps I should somehow get over this conviction or attachment, but of course I cannot and remain honest either to myself or to God.

2

Honest to God or
Honest to Man?

SINCE IT WAS Bishop Robinson whose appeal to honesty and candor sparked so much of the popular interest
in theology today, and since it was he who seriously
suggested the possibility of a "new reformation," it
might be well to consider some of the important
features of his position. Robinson's general thesis is
that it is time for Christians to recognize and accept
the full significance of the secularity of modern man
and reject the traditional picture of a reality that
distinguishes God from this world for a frankly secular and nonsupernaturalist conception of reality. The
new picture does not include the distinction between
the eternal and the perishable. God, or whatever one
wishes to call the transcendent, becomes a quality of
human relations or response, a "ground" or a "depth"
that is not otherworldly but transcendent in Tillich's
special nonsupernatural sense of the term. God is not
a personal Being as such but, as noted earlier, a
quality of life that can best be described as personal
because it manifests love.

Now Robinson and the existentialist theologians reject the idea that they have abandoned objectivity and
divine initiative. Robinson wants to preserve the appearance of objectivity for the sake of keeping his
position credibly Christian. But Robinson and the
existentialists understand objectivity in a special sort
of way best understood, perhaps, by an examination of

Heidegger which I attempt to do later (see pp. 45-46). However persuasive may be their rather subtle redefinition of objectivity, the fact remains that when they speak of an act of God or what God does, they do not mean an objectivity of the sort that is ordinarily supposed. They do not mean, for example, that an independently real personal Being, God, brought about certain things by His divine will. What they mean can only be understood by examining the existentialist's treatment of the subjective-objective issue.

According to Robinson, no particular conception of God is a right or wrong one. But conceptions having their home in the traditional two-world model are uncongenial to modern minds and are increasingly unable to attract new believers or hold old ones. The idea of man as created in God's image is incompatible, he argues, with modern secular man's conception of himself as an evolving creature of nature that has come of age. The whole stance of Christianity, so far as it deals with God or with man, must be reshaped, Robinson argues, if it is to speak to a world for whom the traditional God has died. For most people, he argues, this traditional God "has no connection with what really concerns them day by day." Following Bonhoeffer, Robinson wonders why it is that everyone lives as if there were no God unless it were not for the fact that He is no longer a necessary part of their lives. The secularist is not as mistaken as the Christian has made him out to be. He recognizes those qualities of life that are Christian and accepts them but without the metaphysical baggage that goes with them. Secular man is just as much *inside* the church as out of it, the bishop argues. The old distinction between the redeemed and the unredeemed is simply meaningless if indeed it was ever appropriate.

The bishop's purpose is to speak to those who have, by and large, wanted to believe but could not. It is the release of their great burden—and possibly the bishop's as well—to discover that what they had been expected to believe was not really what Christianity was all about after all. "Robinson is so anxious to persuade himself and others that all good men are 'really' Christians," Mascall writes, "that he invests all his key-words and concepts with both a Christian and non-Christian face and having obtained recognition of the latter, adroitly substitutes the former for it."[1]

But the fact is that what is supposed to be more believable for would-be and can't-be believers turns out to be no more acceptable to the Julian Huxleys and Bertrand Russells than the old Christian beliefs. Indeed, it is less believable if only because it is no longer so clear just what it is that believers are supposed to believe that nonbelievers do not. Indeed it seems that for Robinson and the existential theologians it really does not matter *what* one believes or whether one has any beliefs at all since *that* is not what Christianity is about. The dilemma that faces Robinson and the existentialist theologian, however, is that if "modern man" is the existentialist Robinson thinks he is inclined to be, he will, like Heidegger, revolt against the particularity of a faith centered exclusively in Jesus and opt instead for universalism. On the other hand, if he is as secular as Robinson also believes he is, he will reject any concept of a God including Tillich's as well as classical theism. Hence it will seem to "modern man" that neither God nor Jesus is particularly relevant or even necessary. This is, of course, *precisely* what the conservative characterizes as the blindness of sinful man but what Altizer and the radicals accept as the historical situation today.

Writing in the *Observer*, Julian Huxley spoke of the new language of Tillich used by Robinson as a kind of "semantic cheating . . . so vague as to be effectively meaningless." As far as the atheism of Huxley or Russell is concerned, if there is no God, then there is no God of *any kind* anywhere. To bring Him back as the "ground of being" or as the "beyond in our midst" is

---

[1] Eric L. Mascall, *The Secularization of Christianity*, pp. 161-62.

22

just a sneaky, way of getting back the old-fashioned God or converting nonbelievers by telling them they are really believers whether they like it or not!

Nonbelievers lament that in Robinson the honest atheist is no longer able to recognize as his own the doctrines that were supposed to make him an atheist, and since he never viewed being an atheist as something shameful, he properly resents being told that he is *really* a Christian after all! If he acknowledges that there is such a thing as ultimate reality, an ultimate concern, or a depth of human relationship called love—and he can hardly avoid doing so—he cannot be let off as being the old-fashioned humanist he prefers to be; he must acknowledge that he is with Christ and Christ is with him. To the bona fide secularist or atheist, Robinson appears to be operating a kind of theological fifth column.

Moreover much of what Robinson says is what classical Christian writers have said all along. One does not need Robinson or Tillich to tell him that God is in or at the depth of his being. Nor does he need Bonhoeffer to speak of the Christ who is found in the warp and woof of everyday life. We have always been told this, and in rare and precious moments we have discovered this for ourselves. Robinson is not satisfied merely to restate old truths. He wants us to give up old ways of thinking, if not for our own sakes, then for the sake of others for whom the old images are a snare and a delusion. Even if *we* understand biblical language and Christian beliefs we should be willing to alter them for the sake of those who do not or those for whom these beliefs are an offensive obstacle to the kingdom. Believing that *now* is the day of salvation, the new Christian takes upon himself the task of bringing about the kingdom. "Thy kingdom come, thy will be done, *no matter what*," he prays.

To oppose this kind of argument is difficult because the Christian knows full well that he ought to yield all things to Christ, perhaps some of his cherished ideas as well. And there is something terribly true about the dangers of idolatrous imagery and sterile dogma. Yet

23

there is also something logically odd about trading on ideas whose truth becomes a condition of their rejection. "Where," the philosopher asks, "does Bishop Robinson get his criteria for establishing the character of the gospel?" Who speaks for the gospel? For Christianity?

Let us frankly acknowledge, as we must, that there is a bewildering variety of proposals concerning the nature of the gospel. But does this justify any claim to priority for still another proposal concerning it—this time coming from *outside* the community of belief? Is it a philosophy such as existentialism that is going to serve as the source for the content of the Christian gospel or the norm for its interpretation or intelligibility? Are not Christians *themselves* the proper source of data for any consensus on the gospel or what the Scriptures have to say about it? Robinson and the existential theologians ignore the worshiping and witnessing community of "ordinary believers." It is almost as if for them, the conservative Evangelical did not exist or if he did, he ought not to. But like the famed coelacanth fish caught off South Africa in 1938, the believer goes on living and believing even though he is supposed to have become extinct years ago.

Bertrand Russell once complained that he no longer knew what it meant to be a Christian, since those beliefs that were supposed to identify Christians were often held with greater conviction by non-Christians. No doubt Russell's concern was something less than Christian missionary zeal; yet he was nonetheless justified in demanding some distinguishing characteristics for the Christian God and all the other Christian distinctives.

Now of course Bishop Robinson may speak of God or the gospel in any way he chooses so long as what he says *better portrays* what the Scriptures or what the Christian community have to say. But has he done this? Yes and no. Yes, if some believers and nonbelievers alike have put God somewhere out there in space and need to bring Him down into the depths of their spiritual and social lives. Here Robinson's state-

24

ments would serve primarily to call their attention to certain features of Christian life that have been neglected. As such they would not introduce new rules of use for Christian language. But the answer is no, if "better portrays what the Scriptures and the Christian community have to say" means getting rid of the imagery of the Scriptures and the Christian community or getting rid of a personal God and rewriting Christian beliefs as such.

Robinson says that he does not intend to deprive the Christian of his two-world image with its personal God if this is what the conservative Christian needs to support his faith. But at the same time he says that this image ought to be superseded by Tillichian imagery. But how can Robinson justify his recommendation other than by showing that Tillichian imagery better portrays what believers have believed all along? And he cannot justify his new model solely on grounds of missionary expediency alone; for even if this were a good reason, it by no means follows that the new model *would* communicate better to believers. As a matter of fact it does not and therefore cannot be justified solely on these grounds. Tillich is more mysterious than the Bible for most people—even educated ones—and so far as I know, even Tillichian Christians prefer to sing their songs and pronounce the prayers and benedictions in non-Tillichian traditional Christian language.

Neither does it follow that the old model would not appeal to some nonbelievers since it still does in many cases. The fact that many moderns are rejecting the gospel does not make a case for Robinson either since there have always been rejections of the gospel even when it was proclaimed by Jesus Himself! This has never been a good reason for putting it through a "mutation" or abandoning it.

The argument that historic Christianity no longer finds a hearing among modern men fails for the reason that the gospel never did enjoy an altogether universal response. Christ Himself graphically portrayed the variety of responses His word would receive. There is no particular reason why the gospel should be any more or any less acceptable today than it ever has been and therefore no reason to be particularly surprised at its rejection by so many. Frequent references to the spectacular advances in science are entirely beside the point since they beg the whole question of the relevance of any scientific knowledge to the supernatural activity of God. The bishop's concern looks suspiciously like a rationalization of the failures of liberal Christianity. The problem is not so much one of outmoded world views but of the receptivity of men's hearts and minds, and this is the way it has always been. Even the great philosophical skeptic David Hume recognized that Christian belief could occur only as the result of a miracle wrought by God in the human heart. Contemporary secular man is no more "come of age" than men imagined themselves to be during the Enlightenment or the age of the rational Romans—many of whom were just as sincerely puzzled and repelled by the witness of Christians. Every society and age believes itself to possess the pinnacle of insight and understanding. The Christian knows that only God has this kind of insight and understanding.

Furthermore, "Can a man by searching find out God?" And if not, then what exactly does it mean for a "depth of being" or "ground of being"—whatever these terms may suggest—to take the initiative? In ordinary language, taking the initiative is what a *person* does. It is part of what it means to be a person. Who or what is it for Robinson or the existential theologian that does all those things that God is supposed to do? Can a "ground of being" love, care, or speak to anyone in the way that the Christian God does? Can any God who is not also a person initiate anything—to say nothing of "serving as an agent for redemption"? And if God is not *really* a Person but only a personal response to the whole of things, as Robinson puts it, then what sense is there to a gospel that speaks of a God who "comes in mercy to the wandering sinner and brings him to righteousness"?

Christianity is radical not only because the "beyond is in our midst," to use Bonhoeffer's overworked phrase, but also because the "beyond" *brings it about.* If, as Robinson says, theological statements are only statements about the condition of human life, then what happens to the "mighty act of God in Christ"? Is that a mere figure of speech? Has not Robinson like Feuerbach turned theology into anthropology? After all, he agrees with Feuerbach that the "true atheist is not the man who denies God, the subject; he is the man for whom the attributes of divinity, such as love, wisdom and justice are nothing."[2]

Is Robinson being honest to God or honest to man in the final analysis? Either this is God's world, and we are in some marvelous and mysterious way dependent on Him; or this is man's world to make of it as he will on his own. The secular theologians argue that either there never was a God to start with or, as Altizer says, He died for our sakes, incarnating Himself in the common life of man.

"This is also the paradox with which we are presented in Bultmann," Macquarrie notes. "The method of demythologizing calls for the translation of the New Testament teaching into statements concerning human existence, yet at the same time Bultmann [whom Robinson follows] insists upon speaking of God's decisive act in Christ."[3]

So intent is the bishop on avoiding what he believes to be the superstitious impression that God took a space trip to earth and appeared in the Baby Jesus that he neglects the problem of divine initiative. Yet for him, as for Bultmann and Macquarrie, the *kerygma* of Christian faith must be preserved at all costs. Demythologizing must stop short of scuttling the *kerygma*. But the *kerygma* implies "an activity of God towards man," Macquarrie acknowledges. Even if the "activity of God towards man . . . [is] not merely a past event, but is present wherever the event of Christ

[2] Feuerbach, as cited in John A. T. Robinson, *Honest to God,* p. 50.
[3] John Macquarrie, *The Scope of Demythologizing,* p. 13.

is proclaimed in the *kerygma*," every time a preacher steps behind his pulpit, it is nonetheless and no less an act by someone.[4] And if this "someone" who initiates this "activity" is not part of the natural order, "he" must be super or at least supranatural. What does it mean for Bultmann, Macquarrie or Robinson to speak of "an activity of God towards man" as something more than or objective to what is in or part of the human existential situation? Macquarrie reassures us that "Bultmann ranges himself quite definitely on the side of the New Testament. Christian theology, he believes, must speak not only of a possibility of [authentic] existent [to use Heidegger's phrase] but also of *God's gracious act in Christ* which gives that possibility."[5] The language of biblical supernaturalism is very much in evidence, but the ideas are those of existentialism.

Existentialism must invoke supernaturalism surreptitiously in order to get done what the gospel proclaims. The problem for Bultmann or Robinson or any other existentialist theologian is that so far as he is or can be different from the existentialist *philosopher*, he has to introduce what amounts to the supernaturalism he says he rejects. Either he must be honest to God or honest to man. Much as it might appear that he can be both, he cannot. Either he lets God be God, or he "starts from the other end," as Robinson puts it, and seeks to understand man as he is in his existential situation and speaks of God in these terms and these terms only. Either man is created by God for God's purposes, or God is created by man for his own purposes.

Bultmann, Macquarrie, Tillich and Robinson—to name those thus far mentioned—occupy existential halfway houses between naturalism and supernaturalism. They try to serve God and mammon but neither

---

[4] *Ibid.,* p. 24.
[5] *Ibid.,* p. 25, italics supplied.

will claim them. They try to please both but please neither.

As an existentialist, Bultmann, for example, cannot accept an unequivocally objective God. He puts it this way: "When we speak of an 'act of God', this is not pictorial but analogical language in which 'we represent God's act as *analogous* to a human act."[6] Again this appears to be a satisfactory solution, but to say that an "act of God" is not pictorial is misleading since it suggests that if we take what is said in a nonanalogical way, we must of necessity take it in a pictorial *anthropomorphic* way. We *could,* however, be speaking of God as acting in a way that is neither analogical nor pictorial in the anthropomorphic sense. That is, I could say that as a *matter of fact* God did so-and-so in language *appropriate* to talking about God without at the same time saying that He *acts like man* when He acts or *looks like man* when He acts. I don't have to be bound by any particular *picture of how* God does what He does. The ways of God are for the most part inscrutable to men, but they are not so inscrutable as to preclude our talking about them in the appropriate manner.

Macquarrie clearly recognizes and acknowledges the problem of trying to reconcile attempts to demythologize language about God and attempts to retain a meaningful sense in which one can speak concerning the "acts of God." Bultmann's intention, he writes,

> was to translate all mythical statements into existential statements [i.e., statements about man's existential situation], but . . . there is all the difference in the world between a statement *about* human existence and a statement *in terms of* human existence which is supposed to refer analogously to God [as in talk of an "act of God"]. Either we must say that here there is a limit to demythologizing, or else we must redefine the aim of demythologizing . . . . We are no nearer to having solved the problem of oblique language about God. This problem would have been solved only if

[6] Rudolf Bultmann, as cited in Macquarrie, p. 202, italics supplied.

demythologizing, as purely existential interpretation, had been pursued without limit. This would have meant the abandonment of any attempt to talk about a transcendent God and the representation of Christianity as nothing but a possible way of existence for man. Obviously Bultmann does not want this.[7]

Nor does any occupant of the existential halfway house. But the question is can it be avoided? The answer is, I believe, it cannot. Macquarrie himself acknowledges at any rate that

it seems as if the Christian faith as handed down by the Church is to be dissolved into a philosophy of existence in which one will no longer need to speak of Christ and his work at all, but only of possible ways of being or modes of existence between which men are summoned to decide.[8]

But of course the first long quotation from the end of his book is an answer to the second quotation from the beginning of his book. One cannot take up permanent residence at the existential halfway house without falling back into supernaturalism or pushing on to naturalism.

And in Bultmann also, God is not to be objectified in the usual sense, but neither is He to be subjectified. "He is not just my ideal of myself in the sense in which Sartre can [or Feuerbach does] sometimes speak of God, he comes to me from beyond myself." Although Bultmann seems to be supporting supernaturalism, he is not. "To speak of an act of God," he says, "means at the same time to speak of my own existence."[9] Macquarrie notes, "We recognize him as a being which 'is' beyond our being, but we can speak of him only in so far as he 'speaks' to us in our being."[10] "An act of God is not purely objective," Bultmann continues. "The cross of Christ ... is an

[7] *Ibid.*, p. 215.
[8] *Ibid.*, p. 12.
[9] Bultmann, as cited in Macquarrie, pp. 240-41.
[10] *Ibid.*

30

objective fact of history for everyone, but it is a *saving act of God* only for faith, for the man who makes it his own."[11]

While there is a sense in which one may say what Bultmann says, it nonetheless covers a confusion. If no one "made it his own" would there then be no "saving act of God"? Why is it necessary to mention God at all since the existence of the saving act is contingent only on someone making it his own? Of course there is a trivial sense in which anyone must make it his own in order for it to happen to him, just as for me to see what is before me, I must engage in the act of seeing what is before me. But this in no way alters the objectivity as such of what it is that is seen even if it were to be seen differently. "While we were yet sinners, Christ died for us." Yet it is, of course, only for those who "see" that this is so, that salvation can take place. The redemptive act of God through Christ is there to be appropriated so to speak without regard to whether or not you or I open our eyes to see it.

What the believer must also see is that for the Christian existentialist it is not the person of Jesus who by His resurrection sets men free; it is the *account* of the saving act (that is what it means existentially) that gives rise to it. Jesus is not the living Lord who saves men once and for all but the One who establishes what it means to be a "saved" person. The resurrection is not something that happens to Jesus but something that happens to His disciples and to those who are grasped by its existential significance. On these terms, of course, so far as the resurrection occurs at all it occurs in us. This is clear. But the existentialist uses the platitudinous truth that for something to be significant for us, it must somehow affect us, in order to justify his contention that any other fact about the resurrection is irrelevant and therefore not strictly necessary, for example, that it actually occurred to Jesus in the way described by the

---

[11] *Ibid.*, italics supplied.

New Testament. Like the ancient Gnostic, when he achieves his self-understanding, his personal *gnosis*, it really doesn't matter whether there actually ever was a Jesus who did all of the things He was supposed to have done. The existentialist simply doesn't care what actually happened in the historical, objective sense since what is important for him is what happens in the personal and existential sense. This is necessarily so as we have seen but it is merely a platitude since it would be true in any case.

Macquarrie asks: "What can be meant by saying that the cross is an 'event significant in itself'? For anything to be 'significant' surely it must be *'significant for someone.'* "[12] But he confuses two senses of "significant for someone," significant as it bears upon someone and significant as someone sees that it does. Christ died for sinners whether they know it or not. His act bears upon them, is significant in the first sense above whether or not they see it to be so in the second sense. Macquarrie argues that if the resurrection of Jesus occurred historically " 'outside' believers and 'not in them,' it would not be a 'saving' event but only a historical curiosity."[13] But again Macquarrie confuses the objective redemptive act for the result of appropriating it for oneself. There may be plenty of food for everyone, for example, but for it to nourish anyone, it must be eaten and assimilated by someone. Jesus is the "bread of life" of which we must partake, but even if we do not He is nonetheless available like the uneaten food.

We must answer the existentialist with the argument that the saving event could not occur "in the believer" were it not already an accomplished fact "outside" of him. Hence far from being a historical or cosmological curiosity, the resurrection is a historical and cosmological necessity. Macquarrie mistakenly thinks that if the saving event has not occurred in someone, it has not occurred at all, but of course it only follows that it

[12] *Ibid.*, p. 84.
[13] *Ibid.*, p. 86.

has not occurred in *that* someone; and in saying that, we have not added anything that is not implied in what we already know. The historical saving event is the necessary and sufficient condition of the event "in someone" or "for anyone." Macquarrie writes as though there were a strong disjunction between the saving event as past event on the one hand and the present saving event in someone on the other. But *both* are necessary. There must be both a saving event "outside the believer" and a saving event "inside" him—to use Macquarrie's figures of speech—in order for it to occur "inside." This much should be clear.

In his book, *Sense, Nonsense, and Christianity*, Professor Meynell correctly notes that the claim that it is the *hearing* of the Word and not Christ Himself who supernaturally saves is either trivially true, that is, true by definition, or *probably false*. The proclamation must be supported by historical facts to ensure its meaningfulness as a factual claim. It becomes an empty platitude if supported by definition alone. In an important passage he says:

It is at least arguable that a man may experience a feeling of release from his past and freedom for his future and become morally better (i.e., gain "authentic existence" as the existentialist calls salvation) by listening to the preaching of the Koran or the Buddhist scriptures as well as the New Testament. Once this is granted, if the Word of God is *defined* as that which projects man out of inauthentic and into authentic existence, it follows that either other forms of preaching than that which characterises the New Testament are the Word of God, or it is true merely by definition that freedom from one's past and for one's future is "authentic existence" only when it occurs in response to this particular word of preaching. If the first horn of this dilemma is taken, the uniqueness of the New Testament and the Christ which it proclaims goes by the board, and it must be admitted on Bultmann's premises . . . to be the vehicle of authentic existence, or the Word of God, to Western man in no more proper sense than the Buddhist scriptures are so to the Burmese or Siamese, or the Koran to the Arabs. If the second horn of the dilemma is taken, the sense in which the New Testament is the unique vehicle of the Word of God . . . is a trivial one, a mere matter of definition.[14]

And if it is a mere matter of definition, then it is not factual, and the existentialist's choice to commit himself to the Christian "story" rather than the Buddhist "story" is just that and no more—a voluntary but factually groundless act of commitment designed to give meaning to an otherwise meaningless existence.

Existentialists *reverse* the order of relation between Christ and salvation. Whereas evangelical orthodoxy takes the order to be that given in the fourth gospel or the letters of Paul—in the beginning is the preexistent Son who incarnates Himself and sheds His blood for the salvation of believers—existentialists say instead that "when one experiences atonement [self-understanding or personal *gnosis*] . . . one recognizes Christ as the Word of God."[15] On the existentialist conception of Christ and the resurrection, the reality of Christ is not independent of what happens in persons. If no one achieved "authentic existence," there would be no resurrection, no saving event, indeed no Christ!

The evangelical believer cannot and must not allow himself to be deprived of the facts that give him his hope. Perhaps these facts are supernatural ones, but how else is hope to be sustained? It is not the believer who is nauseated at the sight of the chestnut tree as is Sartre's hero. Existence is not an appalling nothingness for him as it is for the existentialist. It is the gift of a gracious Creator whose living presence endows it with wonder and purpose and whose salvation redeems all things.

[14] Hugo Anthony Meynell, *Sense, Nonsense, and Christianity*, pp. 269-70.

[15] Macquarrie, p. 116.

34

3

Existentialism or
Supernaturalism?

To BE TRULY CHRISTIAN, the existentialist tells us, is
to pursue the secular way of life unencumbered by
supernatural ways of thinking. Of course he means the
secular way of life in the best sense of the term.
Christian faith can survive only as it is understood in
a nonsupernatural existential way, he argues. This is
the Christianity come of age, he says. "Secular theologians share a common presupposition," writes sociologist Peter L. Berger:

> The traditional religious affirmations are no longer
> tenable, either because they do not meet certain mod-
> ern philosophical or scientific criteria of validity, or
> because they are contrary to an alleged modern world
> view that is somehow binding on everybody.[1]

Secular theologians are more likely to embrace atheism than the average theologically untrained skeptic,
Berger says. This phenomenon puzzles believers as
well as sociologists. Why is it that theology appears to
be putting itself out of business?

As a cultural phenomenon, the new secular theology
can be accounted for either as the result of attempts
by liberal theology since Schleiermacher to accom-
modate Christian beliefs to the modern, scientific
world or as the result of the influences upon theology

[1]Peter L. Berger, "A Sociological View of the Secularization of Theology," *Journal for the Scientific Study of Religion* (Spring, 1967), p. 5.

of the forces that account for the modern world itself. Berger writes:

> Secular theology must be understood as emerging from a situation in which the traditional religious certitudes have become progressively less credible, not necessarily because modern man has some intrinsically superior access to the truth, but because he exists in a socio-cultural situation which itself undermines religious certitude.[2]

But the relativizing secular theologian seems to be blind to the relativity of his own debunking maneuvers, he continues:

> What . . . cries out for explanation is the fact that Bultmann and with him the entire movement (of secular theology) takes for granted the epistemological superiority of the electricity-and-radio-users over the New Testament writers . . . . Secularized consciousness is taken for granted, not just as an empirical datum, but as an unquestioned standard of cognitive validity. . . . The question as to who is ultimately right in his knowledge of the world—Bultmann, the electricity-using man in the street, or St. Paul—is . . . bracketed in this perspective.[3]

Secular theologians try "to relativize the religious tradition by means of certain modern ideas," Berger continues, but "these modern ideas . . . can themselves be relativized."[4] It is one thing to identify modernity or what passes for it. It is quite another thing to assert that this modernity is the norm for absolute truth or the absence of it. The fact is that "secularized versions of Christianity . . . rest not upon the rigid applications of the methods of scientific scholarship . . . but upon a radical distaste for the supernatural."[5] If there is any general feature of secular theology which can be iden-

[2] *Ibid.*, p. 10.
[3] *Ibid.*, p. 8.
[4] *Ibid.*
[5] Eric L. Mascall, *The Secularization of Christianity*, p. 282.

tified as something shared by most of that theology as some kind of consensus, it is the forthright rejection of biblical supernaturalism. This is coupled with an inclination to hold that if men are religious by nature, they ought to be religious in a nonsupernatural way as, for example, Tillich says, or to hold as does Bonhoeffer that men are not essentially religious at all and therefore properly Christian when they are secular and nonsupernatural in their beliefs.

It is, of course, entirely gratuitous to assume a priori that the supernatural is impossible or that its descriptions are *necessarily* false since there is nothing logically impossible about supernatural occurrences—no more than there is about *any* occurrences for which descriptions are given that are not self-contradictory.

So far as what modern man can or cannot believe, no safe generalizations can be made. Indeed it is difficult to know what is meant by the abstract term "modern man." According to one study, belief in God may run from a low of 40 percent in certain liberally oriented denominations to a high of 99 percent in more conservatively oriented church groups.[6] These variations are fully as marked if not more so among the leadership of the church. Outside the church the pattern is equally random. The secular theologian cannot justify his program of desupernaturalization on the grounds that supernaturalism is no longer generally tenable, since his own program for substituting existentialism is no less implausible for many others. The fact is that in a pluralistic society such as ours substantial numbers of persons still believe in some kind of a god, more often than not the supernatural God of the Bible. Indeed, the conventions of ordinary speech call for a supernatural theistic God, and while this may sometimes entail a crude anthropomorphism, for most believers it does not. To speak of a "modern world view" that is supposed somehow to be normative simply begs the whole question and ignores the fact

[6] Charles Y. Glock and Rodney Stark, *Religion and Society in Tension.*

that many world views compete for the allegiance of modern man. It also confuses modernity with the "average" outlook which is not necessarily or even more than occasionally scientific as the scientific community itself understands it.

The new apologists try to show, for example, that biblical supernaturalism is one of the vestigial remains of American "folk religion" peculiar to the vanishing American frontier or to a recrudescent Bible belt. But from the fact that some conservative believers may be scientifically or philosophically naïve—and one can hardly deny that they are—it does not follow that they must be. The secularist mistakenly thinks that what the conservative thinks is Christian (i.e., his belief that Christianity has to do with supernatural events) is part of the world view that has gone or ought to go. He assumes that only events of a *natural* kind could occur and that those of a *supernatural* kind could not. Hence he concludes that the believer's belief in supernatural events must be part of a mistaken *natural* world view that must go with it. Now while the language of the believer may be that of a mistaken natural world view, it does not follow that what it is about (i.e., supernatural occurrences) need be either part of that natural world view or mistaken with it. In other words, only the language may be an anachronism and it is simply confused thinking to mistake *this* for the realities to which it refers.

The nature of the case is such that the secular theologian can only offer his program of existential Christianity as an alternative to biblical supernaturalism and theism. He cannot use it to *prove* that biblical supernaturalism and theism are untenable, for he cannot by his own relativistic reasoning show that his program is *intrinsically* superior to that of the supernaturalist. Yet for the secular theologian, "the entire transcendental frame of reference of the Christian tradition is demolished," Berger notes. "It is 'translated into existential anthropology'—a procedure ... of the most radical detranscendentalization and subjectivization imaginable." And radical accommodation of this sort, he argues, tends to "escalate to the point where the plausibility of the tradition collapses . . . from within."[7]

The Evangelical rightly recognizes what the sociologist can see. He opposes secular theology not because he is unable or unwilling to consider new ways of understanding the gospel but because he rightly sees that "ever-deepening concessions to the reality presuppositions of the people one wants to keep or win . . . infect the thinking of the tactitions themselves," and leads to the liquidation of what it was that gave rise to their faith in the first place. Macquarrie himself warns that if "the limit of demythologizing is removed, Christianity ceases to be a religion of saving power and becomes just another view of human existence . . . . It has no longer any gospel and it no longer holds out any hope."[8] But he thinks that demythologizing *can* be cut short without being arbitrary and inconsistent. It is to the credit of the God-is-dead theologians, however, to see that this cannot be done. One cannot leave the household of faith and still remain in it. On this the conservatives and the radicals agree, as opposed to the occupants of the existential halfway house.

The logical conclusion of existential Christianity is the death of God. Note Altizer's startling view that man's final goal is freedom from God Himself. God died for us, Altizer says, so that we can become ourselves. This is not incompatible with the existentialist's conviction that we are wholly responsible for what we are, and we must embrace this responsibility and the anguish it incurs as the mark of our Christian maturity. We must, for example, achieve the self-understanding that is authentic existence. We must understand assertions like "Jesus Christ is Lord and Savior" to mean something nonsupernatural like "I henceforth understand myself . . . solely in terms of

7 Berger, pp. 6, 13.
8 John Macquarrie, *The Scope of Demythologizing*, p. 152.

39

... my encounter with the *kerygma*," as Ogden puts it.[9] And any assertion that Jesus Christ is the only door to salvation must become the claim in existential theology that the nonsupernatural God made known in the event of Jesus Christ is the God who is found everywhere as the universal possibility of authentic existence for all men. From the perspective of the existential theologian, the *kerygma* becomes a kind of existential emancipation proclamation. What was possible for the Man Jesus, we are told, is by its actuality a possibility for us all. And even if there had been no Jesus, what was existentially possible for the early Christians continues to be existentially possible today. And if God *did* choose to die, the least that we can do is to accept His departure gracefully and live forthrightly in a world without God as men come of age.

Secular theologians believe that we are standing at the frontier of a new, post-Christian era and, like Abraham, we must set our sights by a new faith. To look back to the Christian world of the past is to follow the example of Lot's wife. Strategy dictates the abandonment of a thoroughly discredited Bible and of irrelevant supernatural beliefs. The man of faith today is not the man who cherishes the words of the Apostle Paul or those of the fourth gospel as the Word of God. On the contrary, he is the man who moves into the world in a forthrightly secular way to reshape it with the courage and confidence of a man come of age.

The notion of a supernatural God who acts according to His will must be gotten rid of. The word God can no longer be allowed to function in a supernaturalistic way. Talk about God must be seen as talk about man. A viable theology must rely on existentialism rather than on biblical supernaturalism. Existentialism is the philosophical prop of the new theology. It tries to be "honest to man" rather than "honest to God." It translates all theological categories into human categories appropriate to understanding the hu-

[9] Schubert M. Ogden, *Christ Without Myth*, p. 114.

man situation in human terms. Since the human situation is a *present* reality, its symbols and thought forms must be contemporary if they are to be relevant. The Bible no longer qualifies. Its witness is the witness of another age, and its propositions the understanding of that age. Hence, not only biblical propositions but biblical metaphors as well are rejected. Theology must give way to anthropology even as supernatural Christianity must give way to existential Christianity.

Whatever may be the existentialist claims to an objectivity of sorts, the fact is that the desupernaturalizing of theology has been accomplished largely by a subjectivizing of truth. There is a positive correlation between diminishing reference to a sovereign, objective and supernatural God and reference to Christian truth as objective fact. After Kierkegaard and Schleiermacher, it became increasingly fashionable to speak of "truth as subjectivity" as Kierkegaard did, or to reduce God and revelation to special categories of human experience. "Revelation is something which God does," Bultmann insists on saying, but "it is experienced ... [only] in so far as it brings ... a new self-understanding."[10]

What is needed is not propositional truth, a supernatural work of grace, or even a personal God but the possibility of authentic existence. Of course Bultmann and Macquarrie say that this happens only as the gospel is preached and heard as the recognition of the possibility of authentic existence. But it is put in words like "disclosure to us" or "mighty act of God" which lead us to *think* at any rate that what is happening is a revelation of an objective God rather than a subjective illumination. Nevertheless the focus is on the individual and not on God.

When Schleiermacher published his work *On Religion—Speeches to Its Cultured Despisers* in 1799, he made it a point to separate what he took to be the

10 Bultmann, as cited in Macquarrie, p. 226.

41

religious from the factual. He asked whether the religious could be factual in any but a subjective sense, whether such things as the truth claims of the Christian were in any way objective in intention as were, for example, the truth claims of science. To put it in the words of Jenkins:

> We are to find the reality with which religion has hitherto been concerned in an attitude and policy towards the realities of the universe as known to science and the realities experienced in our dealings with the relations between persons. These exhaust the possibilities of reality that there are; and we are told that it is no longer possible to conceive of, still less to have dealings with, reality which is totally different from and transcendent of these realities. God is out, though godly attitudes may be in.[11]

The existentialist theologian says: "Do not multiply entities beyond existential or empirical necessity." Do not introduce or require a supernatural Being, a Trinity, a factual resurrection or anything that is not observable or is not essential to the existential situation. To proclaim the gospel "in terms of the gracious God of the old Reformation ... is not going to match that need," Robinson argues.[12] What will meet that need is to speak of God as a Thou, a Ground, an Ultimate Concern, or simply a Presence. We *can* make sense in this way, we are told. But the existentialist's razor that shaves off the supernatural biblical God makes it possible to speak about things like Tillich's "new being" or Bultmann's "authentic existence" without reference to God at all. Why bother with God or the *kerygma* if we can and do speak of thous, grounds, concerns and presences as transcendent aspects of the human existential situation or the encounter? What is the difference between the existential theologian and the existential philosopher? Buber articulated existential categories beautifully. He was Jewish. Heidegger does not

[11] David E. Jenkins, *Guide to Debate About God,* p. 30.
[12] John A. T. Robinson, *The New Reformation?* p. 52.

even reflect the Judeo-Christian tradition yet he gives us the key to the *kerygma* Bultmann claims. Existentialists talk about the dehellenization of orthodox dogma or the removal of Greek philosophical distortions on the one hand while busily embracing the existentialist philosophical distortions of Buber and Heidegger on the other hand.

The existentialist razor, devised to save the living God of encounter from literal supernaturalism, actually shaves Him off—partly because of a mistaken and unnecessary conception of literal supernaturalism and partly because the existential view of objectivity is hopefully but mistakenly supposed to do what the old classical objectivity did. In this system, the word God is made to function as an adverb or an adjective rather than as a noun. We are to speak meaningfully of godly deeds and godly persons. We cannot speak meaningfully of a biblical "thus saith the Lord." Thus, what started as a move to preserve the living human experience of a personal God finds itself trying and failing, I believe, to keep that experience alive after God has gone. Something strange and unfamiliar takes over from objective faith and belief, and it does not do the job expected of it because it cannot.

Note how Buber makes his point. To speak of an "I" or "Thou" alone, he says, is to speak abstractly, to reduce the I-Thou encounter to an impersonal I-it relationship. The *encounter itself* is what is really real. Whatever may be the transcendent character of the encounter, it is itself what is meant by "God." God is not *in* the encounter. He *is* the encounter. Interpersonal relations give us what we can now refer to as "God" without having to invoke—that is, to abstract—God as a being. As we noted earlier in Robinson, God is the response to all there is *as if* one were being addressed by something personal. Here God is, strictly speaking, the way, the quality or the ground of life—not something abstracted from it. So far as we must use the word God we must use it in this way according to the Christian existentialist, and so far as we do use

43

the word this way, honesty and logic lead us to the God-is-dead conclusion. The end of the road for existentialism is atheism. But it is the philosophers rather than the theologians who have seen this most clearly.

Existentialist theologians try to retain the advantages of supernaturalism while side-stepping its difficulties. When it is desirable to have objectivity in order to speak plausibly of what God does, it points up objectivity. We are reminded that existentialism is not mere subjectivity, and of course strictly speaking it isn't. But neither does it embrace objectivity of the customary kind since that is rejected even more strongly than subjectivism. On the other hand, when it appears that biblical ways of speaking get too anthropomorphic or supernaturalistic, these ways of speaking are disowned and attention is directed to the dynamics of the interpersonal relations or the existential situation instead. This is a clever strategy designed to get as many of the advantages of supernaturalism as is possible without also having to be troubled by its unpopular aspects. And of course there is the perfectly proper sense in which we do try to understand God more adequately, but this is not what I have in mind here. What I have in mind are the nonsupernatural, nontheistic and nonbiblical ways of speaking of God which Evangelicals are obliged to turn aside as unnecessary and distorting accounts of God.

How is it possible, we ask, for the existentialist to speak of objectivity in such a paradoxical way? Why should this puzzling way of speaking improve upon the supernaturalist's verbal attempts to communicate the mystery of God? Two things can be noted. First, paradoxical assertions claiming both objectivity and subjectivity may be used to call attention to the special problem of any attempt to speak of God. In one perfectly legitimate sense, for example, it is entirely in accord with ordinary use to speak of God as promising something. Surely the Christian understands what he believes to be the promises of God. But then are God's promises to be understood as exactly analogous to your promising to meet some friend for lunch? Is God "out there" like another embodied person addressing you with an audible voice? Clearly there is something different about God's promising to stick with us through the valley of the shadow of death and your promising to meet a friend for lunch. Also the Bible speaks of those having "ears to hear." There is a subjective response whose subjectivity is not the same as, for example, our response to what we eat. There is then a point to saying that the paradoxical way of speaking of the existentialist theologian is justified. It does say something in the only way that it can be said. Mystics have claimed this much for a long time.

But there is another sense in which the existentialist's claim to objectivity is confused and seriously misleading. The existentialist speaks of objectivity in the way he does because his concept of objectivity is not the ordinary one. He gets away with it because the nonexistentialist is likely not to detect the existentialist's peculiar use of the term even though he will say, as Macquarrie does for example, that God "is independent of us in not being just a subjective ideal."[13]

To understand how the existentialist can enjoy some of the advantages of claiming objectivity without at the same time having to confront its difficulties and expectations, it will be instructive to examine Heidegger's theory as it is understood and used by Bultmann and discussed by Macquarrie.

Heidegger holds that persons are not isolated souls or subjects related externally to each other and the world generally as though they were prisoners locked up in a body and trying to escape to the outside. On the contrary one is already "outside." We are more like fields of action as, for example, magnetic fields, than like islands. That is why Bultmann says that existence is encounter.

To exist is to know that one does, that is to know oneself as "being-in-the-world." For Heidegger the so-

---

[13] Macquarrie, p. 125.

called philosophical problem of relating an inner subjective self with an outer objective world is spurious. The objective and subjective are already together as a concrete comprehensive unity, a "being there" so to speak, what he calls *dasein*. To distinguish them is to abstract them from the concrete. Macquarrie puts it this way:

> We do not begin with a subject (self) and an object (world) which have somehow to be brought into relation with each other; rather, subject and object, self and world, get sorted out (i.e., abstracted) from the concrete actuality of being-in-the-world.[14]

Heidegger's resistance to any subjective-objective dichotomy is not as such unbiblical. Indeed there is a significant sense in which his view of the world can be said to be biblical. And there is a legitimate sense in which we cannot speak of his or Bultmann's view as a subjective one as, for example, we might speak of Schleiermacher's. The latter was preoccupied with religious experience in a way that the existentialists are not. But we *do* have trouble nonetheless with Heidegger and existentialist theologies like Bultmann's or Tillich's which speak of our being "addressed by" or "grasped by" "gracious grounds" or "gracious beings." These are odd and strained ways of speaking that try to keep the objectivity of theism but try also to escape its tendency to anthropomorphism or tendency as Tillich would say to speak of God as *a being* among other beings. I shall not attempt to discuss Tillich here.

For Heidegger and existentialists generally, truth is not a property of propositions in the usual sense of speaking of propositions that are factual. Truth is part of what it is to exist. Getting to know anything is not discovering something outside ourselves because we are already "in-the-world." Hence it is more like acquiring self-understanding. So far as we do exist and exist *authentically* our "being-in-the-world" is re-

[14] *Ibid.*, p. 192.

vealed or disclosed to us. To exist and to understand oneself are one and the same thing because to exist *is* to understand that we do, that is to stand in the presence of reality revealed.

Now let us apply this complex but influential idea to the gospel as does, for example, Bultmann. For the existential Christian the resurrection event is the self-understanding that arises in the encounter, in his response to reality. "Everything else in the gospels is a mythological embroidering of it."[15] There is no objective sacred history, no beginning or end of time, no supernatural historical incarnation of God in Christ, no resurrection into glory. Everything coalesces into the mysterious encounter that seems to be God, the resurrection and eternal life together at once. It is the existentialist's "happening" that is somehow immune to logical penetration. Herein lies the basic incompatibility of existentialism and supernatural biblical Christianity. For the existentialist there is an *original* possibility of authentic existence for everyone in his particular historical situation that is itself historical and universal. Jesus exemplifies that possibility. For Christians this possibility is not merely exemplified by Jesus but comes into being through what He does for us. He and He alone is the Author of our salvation. It is what He does and not what He illustrates that saves us.

The new existentially interpreted God is not the supernatural God of biblical Christianity. He is a kind of *tertium quid,* a third something that is neither the old-fashioned God of orthodox objectivism nor the numinous religious experience of liberal subjectivism. This is why non-Christians see this "new" God as no God at all. They wonder why He should be so mightily championed when needed to "save mankind" but renounced when not needed as an outmoded anachronism. Robinson regrets that he "cannot agree with the reviewer [of his book] in the *Indian Journal of Theol-*

---

[15] *Ibid.,* p. 270.

47

ogy that 'if this interpretation of Christianity were to prove true, it would mean the end of the mission of Christianity.' "[16] But the fact is that the Hindu reviewer of Robinson's *The New Reformation?* is precisely right just as Professor Altizer is also precisely right about halfway existential positions like Robinson's. They cannot succeed because they have *already* abandoned what they set out to defend. Notions like "being itself" or "the encounter" that serve as a third "something" introduce a kind of *philosophical* anthropomorphism. God is conceptually rather than physically manlike. These philosophical categories obscure and distort the God who *does reveal Himself*. They do not clarify Him since only He Himself can do this in His own way. They fulfill the Gnostic's urge to make over God into what is intellectually tolerable or what will give one a satisfactory self-understanding. The myth embodied in biblical imagery is broken, but it is replaced by a philosophical substitute that is no less idolatrous than the golden calf of the Israelites.

The problem with existential theologians like Bultmann is that so far as he is to be any different from existential philosophers who have no *kerygma*, he is obliged to introduce what amounts to supernaturalism. In limiting demythologizing to all but the gospel, he satisfies neither believer nor unbeliever. Macquarrie acknowledges that "it has to be admitted that Bultmann sometimes speaks as if the doctrines of Christianity could be reduced entirely to statements about the possibilities of human existence."[17] Elsewhere he also admits that "Bultmann's approach to the New Testament is ... frankly anthropological, and for him the history of salvation is the unveiling of a possibility of human existence."[18]

Even if one grants that Bultmann is not saying that the possibilities of one's own existence can be achieved

[16] Robinson, p. 13.
[17] Macquarrie, p. 127.
[18] *Ibid.,* p. 119.

solely by one's own efforts, it does not follow that what he says is distinctly Christian. The philosopher can also hold for a kind of *nonchristian* grace, that is, something beyond what man can do for himself that is not Christian at all. Macquarrie paraphrases Buri's objection to Bultmann:

> If we follow Bultmann in interpreting the cross existentially how does that differ from that "turning from the world" of which philosophers speak without reference to the cross of Christ? ... It is not [even] necessary that philosophers should think of authentic existence as something to be attained by man's own powers. The idea of grace is not exclusively a Christian idea.[19]

Bultmann's Christian existentialism may look like a philosophy to the believer, "but to philosophers themselves," Macquarrie says, "he appears as just another myth-maker because of his appeal to the *kerygma*."[20] Bultmann's halfway position leaves him clinging to just enough Christianity to make him unacceptable to radicals like Buri or Van Buren but not enough Christianity to satisfy other "halfway" thinkers like Brunner—to say nothing of evangelical believers.

Bultmann wants to translate all of what he calls the "mythical" statements of the New Testament into existential statements. But if he cannot solve the problem of language about God by demythologizing unless he must also demythologize the gospel too, "this would mean the abandonment of any attempt to talk about a transcendent [supernatural] God and the [consequent] representation of Christianity as nothing but a possible way of existence for man.[21] And even if he were successful in preserving an exclusively existential gospel, he would still not know whether he was mistaken in rejecting the supernatural gospel after all.

[19] *Ibid.*, p. 134.
[20] *Ibid.*, p. 135.
[21] *Ibid.*, p. 215.

49

Professor Hepburn is right when he says:

> Overwhelmingly concerned with the phenomenology of
> faith and the life of faith, existential thought is in
> continual peril of failing to emerge from the subjec-
> tivist circle at all. A subjectivist account can provide
> an informative description of what it is like to think
> and act *as if* there was a God . . . . But it is unable to
> go further . . . and say whether the belief is justified
> or unjustified, whether or not there exists a being be-
> fore whom the believer has taken up the attitude of
> faith.[22]

And Professor Macquarrie is also right when he says:

> If the New Testament message is to be reinterpreted
> not only with regard to the modern world-picture but
> also with regard to the modern self-understanding,
> then there can be no place for a *kerygma* in it . . . . In
> the biblical self-understanding man is a creature *de-
> pendent upon God*. There can be no possibility of try-
> ing to reinterpret the New Testament message in a
> way which would accommodate [the] average modern
> self-understanding . . . . such a presentation falls far
> short of biblical teaching. Sin is not just alienation
> from oneself, it is alienation from God. Authentic
> existence is not just coming to oneself, it is coming to
> God.[23]

But Macquarrie wants all this on *existentialist* terms—
an existentialist view of God, of objectivity, of the
gospel, and of authentic existence. The question is
how can what he says be true short of acknowledging a
New Testament supernaturalism.

It is evident that Macquarrie fully recognizes
Bultmann's difficulties, but he believes they can be
resolved without embracing supernaturalism. This has
not been demonstrated. What is needed is not demythologizing or an existential *kerygma* but an approach

[22] As cited in Antony Flew and A. Macintyre (eds.), *New Essays in
Philosophical Theology*, pp. 237-40.
[23] Macquarrie, pp. 235-36, italics supplied.

to the New Testament unburdened with conclusions made up in advance about what can and cannot happen and a different conception of language. It would not hurt either to display more confidence in the biblical authors and in the ability of God Himself to make known His Word for us.

4

Is There Propositionless Revelation?

I HAVE ALREADY REFERRED to the influential idea that religious truth is existential rather than propositional and that Christianity is not a supernatural revelation but a way of life. The view that religious truth is exclusively existential and that neither revelation nor religious experience can provide a source of information in any of the usual senses of the term is advanced for several reasons. The main reason seems to be that religious truth cannot qualify as empirical knowledge or knowledge in any of the usual senses of the term. Hence it must be a special kind of knowledge that is nonpropositional, personal—a direct acquaintance of some sort. Knowledge of God, it is said, is more like knowing oneself or one's wife. It is too intimate to be communicated. It is "lived" or "experienced" rather than propositional truth. It simply cannot be communicated in propositional form.

There are, of course, some things about oneself or one's wife that are literally inexpressible. But it does not follow that nothing can be known about myself, my wife or God, or that I cannot communicate facts about myself, my wife or God. Certainly it does not follow that God *cannot* communicate facts about Himself. His "concealedness" does not preclude propositional communication, and His "unconcealedness"—to use Heidegger's term—strongly suggests propositional communication.

The existential theologian insists, however, that God discloses Himself rather than information about Himself. He is known existentially as encounter we are told. Of course I would not want to deny that God does disclose Himself since this would be to deny one of the most important Christian truths. But I would want to say that because we *do* know things about Him we *can* say that He discloses Himself. These are things that we *do* put propositionally. These must be included with things that cannot be put propositionally. For example, I know and state unequivocally that God cares for me. Why He should is something else. The love of God is inexpressible. If God can disclose Himself at all, He is able to disclose propositions about Himself. Surely one would not want to say that God deliberately limits Himself so as to prevent propositions from getting revealed! Hence either there is propositional revelation or there is no revelation at all. I cannot conceive of any personal self-disclosure that is not also a propositional disclosure.

There is, of course, a difference between saying that the encounter is personal in the trivial sense of saying that any experience of encounter must of necessity be someone's experience, and saying that the encounter is personal in the significant sense of saying that the encounter is personal in the significant sense of saying something about it, that is, for example, giving information about it to the effect that it is personal. If the latter is claimed, then it is hardly possible to know God without also knowing something about Him if only that which has to do with the way He reveals Himself. And if we insist on using personal pronouns, our assertions will become suspiciously like those that we make concerning anything whatever that we claim to know. From the very fact that we want to say that He discloses Himself there is strongly suggested the fact that there is something about the disclosure that gives us good reason to talk in this particular way.

I do not believe that the encounter theory as it is advanced, for example, by Bultmann or Brunner adequately supports the contention that religious truth is wholly existential, that it is merely a self-understanding—however profound may be the insight of the existentialist. On the contrary I shall contend that religious truth must be both existential in the appropriate sense *and* propositional. Indeed any truth that is without propositional content hardly qualifies as truth on the existentialist's own terms. Even Heidegger's truth as "unconcealedness" implies propositional content, and he explicitly acknowledges this. Concerning his view of truth, Macquarrie says that "to understand the 'truth' of one's existence, to have this existence 'unconcealed,' is also to penetrate into the *understanding* of being, into the mystery of God."[1] But what can be *understood* that is propositionless? If what the existentialist said *were* true he couldn't *know* that it was or *say* that it was.

Plato speaks of a knowing without saying. In the final sense, the mystery of God or, for that matter, mortals too is not fully expressible. Who can express or even conceive the love of God or even human love? But does this mean that nothing can be known or said concerning it? This is like arguing that we cannot say anything unless we can say everything or like arguing that we cannot know anything unless we can know everything. It is what we *do* know and *can* say rather than what we do not know or cannot say that gives specific content to our faith in Jesus Christ, and this is not at all to say that we exhaust His mystery.

One wonders why a supernatural, sovereign God—if He exists—would confine or restrict Himself to a propositionless self-disclosure even if He could. Why should He compromise the content of the Scriptures? If the Scriptures do as much as Brunner and Bultmann want them to do, they should do much more. Either there is propositional revelation or there is no revelation at all, since any God who disclosed

[1] John Macquarrie, *The Scope of Demythologizing*, p. 219, italics supplied.

Himself would also disclose propositions about Himself. Indeed one would think that a God who cared as God is supposed to, would do just what believers believe He did, that is, reveal Himself propositionally as well as personally in the written Word.

Those who hold for a propositionless revelation are not limiting themselves with regard to what they can say. They are limiting God. Now where it actually exists, bibliolatry is rightly condemned by Brunner and all who repudiate evangelical Christian belief, but this condemnation in no way justifies the idolatrous *philosophical* anthropomorphism put in its place. God's revelation cannot be restricted so as to say that orthodox beliefs could not be true on any terms. What one can or cannot say about God works both ways. If one cannot say that God would not reveal Himself once and for all, so that one can say that He does reveal Himself in many and continuing ways, then one cannot say that He does not reveal Himself once and for all either. The question is not what God could not do as the existentialist wants to say but what He *does* do as the believer says, and believers say that God does both reveal Himself once and for all in the incarnation *and also* in many and continuous ways. They also say that He discloses *Himself* in the *person* of *Jesus Christ* while at the same time disclosing *facts* about what He has done, what He expects us to do, and so on. It is the existentialist who idolatrously claims to know what God is not or what God cannot do. He is not this or that, and He cannot do this or that, we are told. It is the existentialist who limits God.

"Liberalism," Macquarrie argues, "is never final, for it recognizes a hiddenness in transcendence beyond what man can grasp."[2] This much can certainly be said. But what if God *were* to make a final self-disclosure? *Can* we say that He cannot do this or would not do this? How does the liberal or the existen-

[2] Macquarrie, p. 151.

tialist know that God has not done just this? I am not appealing to ignorance and claiming that the liberal's inability to demonstrate what he claims, proves the truth of the believer's claims. The believer doesn't claim proof of God's revelation *in this way*. His authority is the whole revelation itself. What I am saying is that the liberal confuses the "radical openness" of faith for the fact that God does or does not do certain things. From the fact that if there is a God, He is no doubt an inexpressible mystery, it does not follow that He cannot or would not disclose Himself in the concrete and final way claimed by the believer. Having done this, God could remain fully as inscrutible as anyone could want Him to be, that is, truly a *deus absconditus*. This is what the believer claims— not that in disclosing Himself in a concrete, historical and propositional way, God loses His depth and mystery.

The rejection of propositional revelation by Chrisian existentialists is best understood in the light of their "truth as encounter" theory. This theory is probably best approached by way of an examination of Buber's influential exposition of it. According to Buber, human existence has two forms: relation as I-Thou and connection as I-it. Most of human existence has the I-it character, but it is the I-Thou relation that gives it significance. I-Thou relations are possible only when one encounters something in a personal way. For Buber this need not mean encountering persons only, since one can "encounter" anything. We noted earlier that Robinson spoke of God as that quality of things that calls forth a personal response in us.

I-Thou is what is meant by being human, that is experiencing hope and despair, guilt and forgiveness, love and hate, acceptance and rejection, and so on. Compare Bultmann's "authentic existence" or Tillich's "new being." It is not so much a human achievement as it is a kind of human existence. It is what Buber means by being in God or having God in us. Although he specifically rejects mysticism as do most existential theologians, I do not see that the I-Thou can be described as anything short of the mystic's identification in depth with the reality to which he opens himself.

But whatever it is, the I-Thou relation is, as we already noted in Bultmann, the normative form of human existence, how we ought to exist, what it means to have self-understanding. Indeed it is claimed to be what knowing God is, so far as the existentialist wants to include reference to God at all. What is especially important is that Buber wants to stress relation or "betweenness"—the hyphen in the I-Thou, so to speak—rather than abstractions like "I" or "Thou" as such. It is the I-Thou encounter itself that is what we mean by existential truth, indeed what we mean by God.

The existentialist does not use the word "truth" in the customary sense of meaning "true" statements but in the substantive sense of meaning a state of human existence. By saying both that existence is encounter and that truth or even God is encounter, Buber is able to refer to a truth that is both substantive as a possible state of human existence and substantive as revelation so far as God encounters man. By being both revelation and truth, encounter can be something that is—hopefully at least—purely existential, nonpropositional and without reference to an objective Being, God. Both God and propositional truth as they are ordinarily understood are given up for the encounter. The encounter substitutes for God—what He says or what can be said about Him. Faith, hope and love are not distinct things to be talked about as though they could be described or articulated in terms of true propositions. They are part of our self-understanding itself. We are instructed to "existentialize" our faith—not "intellectualize" it.

No doubt many Christians lay claim to propositions which modesty alone should keep them from asserting, and there can be no doubt that the work of the Holy

Spirit is claimed when it should not be. But these excesses in no way justify the notion that a religious truth claim can be exclusively existential. Nor is the claim that Christian truth is somehow different from other truth a justification for the claim that it is nonpropositional. This strategy of the existentialist is simply an instance of special pleading.

Existentialists endow the encounter with extraordinary attributes. Buber says, for example, that to address any particular "thou" in an encounter is to address God—the eternal "Thou." This can be taken to mean either that God is pointed to in I-Thou relations or that the I-Thou is what is meant by God or both. Since Buber does not want to abstract the "Thou" from the I-Thou, he can have a "Thou" or God only in the sense that by God both of these things are meant.[3] He does not intend to reduce God or encounter to mere feeling. Even though feeling is, he says, "ever so essential," it is nevertheless "a mere accompaniment to the relation," that is, the encounter.[4] "The dialogical situation," he says elsewhere, "can be adequately grasped only in an ontological way. But it is not to be grasped on the basis of the ontic of personal existence, or of that of two personal existences, but of that which has its being *between them* and transcends both."[5]

Here there is what I suggested earlier in Bultmann, a *tertium quid*, a third something that is neither you nor me nor God as Person but something else. Now the classic Christian position is that all three are at least equally important—the person who is in relation to other persons and to God, the God "in whom we live and move and have our being," and the supernatural grace which reconciles us all one to the other and to God through Christ. The price that any existential theologian pays for rejecting classical Christianity is the reduction of the reality of both God and man to

[3] Martin Buber, *I and Thou*, pp. 6, 63, 75, 101.
[4] *Ibid.*, p. 81.
[5] Buber, *Between Man and Man*, p. 204, italics supplied.

the reality of the encounter that relates them. He mistakenly believes that by deemphasizing the "I" and the "Thou," he is able to (1) keep them from becoming I-its, and (2) preserve the existential vitality of the relationship as such. He is mistaken because he confuses the *logical* distinction we must make between ourselves as persons and the person of God for the distinction that makes us into isolated island things. There is no reason why we cannot *speak* of real persons and a real God without at the same time being guilty of abstracting them from living relationships. I can refer to my wife as a concretely distinct and real person without at the same time jeopardizing my relationship with her. I can refer to God as concretely real and distinct in the person of Christ without jeopardizing my relationship to Him or *in* Him if the existentialist prefers. It is the existentialist who by idolizing that relationship jeopardizes it. The strategy designed to preserve the I-Thou encounter tends to remove the reason why it should be preserved. Indeed if the I-Thou encounter can characterize my relationship with a tree as well as another person—as Buber claims it can—I am already suggesting that the existence of persons as such—to say nothing of the person of God—is secondary to existence as encounter. The encounter becomes an idolatrous substitute for persons and for God. In trying to keep alive the encounter in this way, the existential theologian actually tends to destroy it.

Even if Buber and other existentialists did manage to keep sight of what is related, their followers did not always succeed nor did they always try. They took the eclipse of God seriously if not as literally as did Buber. And if Buber and the existentialist theologians do manage to escape the mysticism they eagerly renounce, their escape is academic, for even if they could preserve some semblance of God, they would still confine themselves to existential religious truth. It is to this problem that we must again turn, and it is Brunner's treatment of it that will get our attention.

Brunner makes full use of Buber's I-Thou idea. For

59

him, revelation is the divine-human encounter rather than disclosure of propositions about God. Clearly he strives to preserve God's objective and personal reality in a way that others like Tillich find unnecessary if not impossible. He considers the divine-human encounter to be the most fundamental category of the Bible. Propositional revelation seriously compromises this fundamental category, he believes. Yet if truth is simply encounter and nothing more—as Brunner says it is—if "truth as idea"—propositional truth—is Greek and unbiblical, one should hardly be surprised to find later existential theologians arguing that "truth as encounter" implies *no particular ideas at all*—not even a meaningful use for the word "God."

The same razor that Brunner used to shave off literalism is used to shave off what remains of biblical ideas that were still firmly part of his own thinking. With existential truth, theology is free to consider any beliefs or no beliefs at all as Christian. Novelty is interpreted as evidence of spiritual renewal and vitality. And we are told that Christian beliefs must change if they are to remain Christian. Brunner compromised the very thing that could ensure preservation of the encounter—belief in the concrete spiritual reality of the person of God as expressed in "truth as idea."

What about doctrine? Is it able to deter the extravagances of the existentialists? No, for the reason that doctrine is pictured as the symbolic vehicle of the encounter. The Scriptures point to, or witness to, revelation. They are not themselves revelation, since propositions about God—who He is, what He is like, what He has done, or what He commands and promises—are not the Word of God. What God *says* is not the Word. God communicates only Himself as encounter we are told. The Word is restricted to that.

But it seems clear to me that the Bible itself amply substantiates its claim to what God *says* as well as to what points to Himself. Brunner wants to say that "God's way of 'speaking' has changed from the literal 'speaking' [through the prophets]: it has become," he says, "a more figurative way of 'speaking.' "[6] So apprehensive is Brunner of compromising the existential character of truth, of compromising the fact that God speaks in Jesus Christ, that he wants to restrict God's revelation of Himself to the existential alone. Revelation, he contends, *is* the encounter. It is not a body of information. But if the response of existential faith in encounter with God is the response of the whole person to the whole of God's personal self-disclosure, then how could it be that information is no part of it? How is it possible for any *intelligible* revelation to exclude it? Even if there were no revelation as the written Word of Scripture, the revelation of encounter could not be propositionless as Brunner and existentialists want to say.

If propositional revelation is unavoidable in principle as part of any revelation as encounter or any revelation whatever, it must also be part of that revelation that gets into written symbols as well. Surely if God can use men for nonpropositional purposes, He can also use men for uttering propositions. The fact that determining *what* God uses them to say may be difficult to arrive at does not demonstrate that God has not said anything—if indeed it is as difficult as it is made out to be. Some things seem to be *very clear* to those whose hearts are open to what God is saying, and I would have thought that it was the task of theology to aid this task rather than to obfuscate it.

Yet two things are held against the position I have just taken. It is held, for example, that to say what I have just said misunderstands and misrepresents revelation. When God speaks, Brunner argues, He speaks with and through Jesus Christ. The person of Jesus *is* the message. The invitation to new life—not information—is the good news. According to Brunner, to say "I believe" is not to say something like "I believe the earth is round." It is to say something like "I accept"

• H. Emil Brunner, *Dogmatics, I: The Christian Doctrine of God*, 23.

or "I trust," and so on. But how can *this* be said without that which gives it form and substance?

The Bible gives ample evidence of the rich propositional as well as nonpropositional character of all revelation. Its use of imagery and virtually all of the verbal devices for communication is evidence of propositional disclosures—not evidence against it. Symbols convey propositional as well as existential truth. Peter's witness "Thou art the Christ" is, for example, also, but not limited to, the proposition "He is the Christ." When we witness we also inform. No doubt some literalists have given too much attention to the informative features of the words they read and have neglected other, and perhaps more important, features. Nonetheless the existentialist mistakenly thinks he communicates propositional truth as part of his confession of faith only by killing that confession. That, it seems to me, is a more serious mistake than the mistake of some believers who neglect some features of Christian utterances for others.

Another mistaken belief about propositional revelation is its alleged incredibility. Existentialists tend to assume that anything that the Bible says that is spiritually or supernaturally informative is no longer credible. Hence if one can show that what the Bible *appears to say* is not necessarily what God is saying today or what He ever did say, then the problem of incredibility is solved. This strategy fails on two counts. First, what the existentialist offers as a substitute is no less incredible to many would-be believers. Second, formless "truth as encounter" can and has taken on whatever form one may wish to give it, and there is virtually no limit to the ingenuity of the human mind when it comes to religious speculation.

Trust, obedience and love must be emphasized, Brunner says, rather than doctrine. But is doctrine or "truth as idea" incompatible with any of these? Need "truth as idea" give way to "truth as encounter"? For that matter, can it? It is simply a mistake to think that the latter can be preserved by abandoning the former. It is the mistake of thinking that there is any such thing as encounter without idea. Not only is there no such thing as "truth as encounter" without "truth as idea," but it is only the latter that can be properly spoken of as truth at all in the ordinary sense. "Truth as encounter" or "existential truth" refers to something altogether different from what is ordinarily meant by truth. These terms are persuasive redefinitions of the word "truth" for the purpose of associating it in a favorable way with what one wants to identify as the vital element of religious experience. And of course one wants to say that there is such a thing as religious experience. It *is* of supreme significance, but so is that which enters into it, the real persons who confront a real God. Contemporary theology is trying to keep alive that experience in the face of the fact that it can no longer believe in Him who gave rise to it in the first place.

Buber's explicit concern is to keep alive what he calls "the disclosure of the Presence." He goes so far as to say "it is not necessary to know something about God in order really to believe in Him."[7] But what possible meaning can the expression "believe in Him" have under these circumstances?

An important corollary of the doctrine that truth is encounter is the doctrine that truth is transitory. Since encounter is transitory, revelation is also said to be transitory. The truths of revelation are the particular encounters themselves. The responses of faith are the particular responses of the *situation*. This is a situational theology. The Word of God is the revelation of the moment or situation. It is authorized by the claims of the encounter rather than by any external or absolute standard. Its truth is not something that can be shared as objective information to which several may give witness. Its truth can only be existentially shared. Hence the symbols of the Christian service of

[7] Buber, *The Eclipse of God,* p. 40.

worship, for example, may mean different things and serve different functions for the worshipers. There is nothing that the community of faith shares that is as such canonical. "The Word of God," says Buber, "crosses my vision like a falling star to whose fire the meteorite will bear witness without making it light up for me, and I myself can only bear witness to the light but not produce the stone and say 'This is it.'" Further, "there is not the slightest assurance that our decision is right in any but *a personal way.*" The truth of encounter "needs to be discovered ever anew."[8]

The encounter or existential view of truth is the key, I believe, to the understanding of the new theology. But it is also the Achilles heel of that theology, for it is in the analysis of the encounter itself that we discover why the existential theory of truth fails. Brunner, for example, is convinced that those who equate the Bible with the Word of God have infected Christian thought with nonbiblical intellectualism. He rejects verbal inspiration. Truth is encounter or existential—not propositional. God discloses Himself, not facts about Himself. The Scriptures are not the authority for Christian truth but "the source of all that truth which possesses absolute authority."[9] But he also acknowledges that "we can never separate the abstract framework from the personal Presence contained in it," and it is also apparent that he does not wish to diminish the importance of correct doctrine. However, he sees the doctrinal or propositional elements as something that *follow* the encounter rather than as constituting part of it.[10] And it is apparent that those who follow him, the later generations of existential theologians, *do* diminish the importance of correct doctrine even as they *do* diminish the importance of a personal God or the supernatural and objective character of His acts. Again it is not altogether

[8] Buber, *Between Man* . . . , pp. 7, 69, italics supplied.
[9] *Ibid.*, p. 47.
[10] Brunner, *Truth as Encounter*, p. 132.

what Brunner says that is in itself unacceptable but rather what it leads to. If there is no way of judging doctrinal responses to encounter, then there is no way of establishing any particular content as normative. We *do* live by faith, but this faith is supported by specific beliefs. It is not an irrational confidence of some kind *no matter what*.

How, we ask, is it possible to reassure ourselves that the Christ to which the Bible gives witness will remain that very Christ that confronts us in the face of no abiding truths about Him? Even more serious is the question whether that very same God who does disclose Himself as the living God in Christ does not or is not able to complete that disclosure in such a way that the knowledge thus revealed will be the sufficient condition for the salvation of all who believe.

Since the existentialist models the divine-human encounter on the interpersonal encounter, let us examine that encounter to see whether self-disclosures are as propositionloon as the existentialist makes them out to be. Let us take the encounter of a man with his wife as our paradigm case. He "knows" his wife in many ways. These ways disclose facts about her. They include facts that are not explicitly stated as well as some that may be communicated in written form. He sees that her hair is red. He knows of her love in all that she does or does not do. Clearly he knows a great deal despite the great deal that he does not know or is mistaken about. Does the analogy break down because God is spiritual? But then is not human intimacy spiritual as well as physical?

A common argument against propositional revelation is that it leads to a sterile intellectualism or unimaginative literalism. This argument is fallacious. It is like arguing that because there is a danger of overeating or even getting poisoned, we should refrain from eating altogether. If God's self-disclosure is at least as much as human self-disclosure, we should avail ourselves of whatever that encounter can communicate to us in whatever form God chooses to reveal

Himself. Unless we do partake of the Bread of Life—
however risky it may be for some—we may not survive
to do anything else.

Another common error is the misunderstanding of
logic. Brunner's case is typical. He thinks that the
application of logic necessarily corrupts existential
Christian faith. His mistake arises from his failure to
note that logic applies to our thinking and talking
about God, not to God Himself necessarily. Even if
God's own nature were logically problematical so that
logic was inapplicable, this would not imply that we
could scrap it in *our* thinking or speaking of Him. We
have to be intelligible in our speaking of anything—
even the inscrutable. It is one thing to say that whatever I say about God must proceed according to the
rules of logic in order to be intelligible for me or
anyone else and quite another thing to say that the
rules that apply to my concepts and reasoning must
also circumscribe the mystery of God.

The lack of regard for logic that characterizes the
thinking of some of the existential theologians is
reflected in their misuse of paradoxes. There is a difference between trying to depict a real mystery which
may properly call for the use of paradoxical expressions
and attributing the paradox to the mystery. The world
is simply what it is. It is not per se paradoxical since
only expressions are paradoxical. The may may be
distorted but not the world it represents. Our expressions may be paradoxical but not what they refer to
except insofar as they are self-referring as part of the
world themselves. Hence to speak of God as paradoxical because He is mysterious is simply misleading. If He were paradoxical, we could not know that
He was. We could only know that we have to speak of
Him in a paradoxical way. But this would only hold
so far as certain obscure or puzzling features of God
were concerned, and the paradoxical expressions would
be used to call attention to *those* features, not all
features. We may have to speak paradoxically about
God's being. To a question like Is He *a* Spirit? we

might want to answer by saying yes and no. But to a question like Does He care? we would prefer an unequivocal yes! This is why symbols and images may be preferred. The paradox may serve as one of these. But to think that being paradoxical is a special virtue of God or that logic is an enemy of faith is to misconstrue the whole question.

Some theologians refuse to abide by the very rules that scientists and everyone else are obliged to follow in order to make sense. They do this for the curious reason that they think the object of their inquiry will be compromised if they speak of it in an intelligible manner. But if God's Word is available to children and savages, surely it should be available to the theologian; and if it is available, it is available in intelligible terms.

The truth as encounter doctrine fails to account for the actual nature of encounter and dangerously impoverishes the idea of revelation. Singling out existential truth as the only truth of revelation fails to preserve that very truth. Indeed to single it out as the whole truth is to abstract it from the whole of God's revelation. When God encounters man, His self-disclosure is no less propositional than any ordinary encounter. God as person is no less real and concrete in the spiritual sense appropriate to Him than the reality of any person. When existential theologians say that the propositions of the Scriptures only point to revelation, we must say that they point to revelation as God's self-disclosure only because they are themselves part of that disclosure as the written Word. And when they say that the encounter calls for our response in a personal way, we must say that we respond in a personal way only because the divine person of God addresses us as persons created in His image. When they speak of anthropomorphism, we must speak of theomorphism. And when they look at what man is saying, we must look at what God is saying.

5

What About Truth?

THE WORD "truth" is a substantive, an abstract noun.
When one speaks of the truth with the intention of
endowing it with its full ontological significance, one
might, as did the biblical writers or Saint Augustine,
refer to God Himself or to His Word. We speak, for
example, of Christ Himself as we did above as truth.
We can also speak of truth in its adjectival function.
Here "true" refers to the relation between words or
ideas and the world or whatever is the case. We speak,
for example, of true beliefs, true statements, true assertions, true propositions, or simply "truths" when
certain specific conditions are met; and of false statements, false assertions, false propositions, and so on,
when these conditions are not met.

These conditions depend on the kind of assertion
which one wants to characterize as true or false.
Words like "true" may be used in a commendatory
way by which we commit ourselves to certain beliefs or
ascribe value to a certain doctrine, but they need not
be so used. Often the criteria or requisite conditions of
truth or true belief include verification in some form.
But to think that verifiability or falsifiability as philosophers usually speak of them are the only criteria,
or to think that they are employed in a uniformly
empirical way is to mistake the criteria for some kinds
of truth or true belief for the criteria that may be
required of all truths or true beliefs.

What seems to characterize all true statements is
that they involve a special relationship between what

is thought or said and some state of affairs. They refer both to what is thought or said and *also* to a state of affairs. A statement cannot without absurdity refer to itself. And what determines its truth cannot be some feature of the statement alone. No matter how passionately I may hold my belief, no matter how cleverly I may articulate it, its truth cannot be settled merely by any feature of the belief alone or by how I hold it.

"When a statement is true," the philosopher Austin argued, "there is, *of course*, a state of affairs which makes it true and which is *toto mundo* distinct from the true statement about it; but equally of course, we can only describe that state of affairs *in words* . . . . I can only describe the situation in which it is true to say that I am feeling sick by saying that it is one in which I am feeling sick."[1]

It is the common thing to speak of truth as a property of beliefs and statements. Under what conditions, we ask, would the belief, for example, that Jesus Christ is Lord and Saviour be true? Ordinarily we will say "When it corresponds to the facts." And there is nothing inherently wrong with saying that, although the philosopher will want to know exactly what it was that was said or done in making the assertion and exactly what conditions were met or would have to be met for it to be true. He is entitled to know what these conditions are but not to prescribe them. These are the conditions in terms of which it is appropriate to describe a certain expression as true.

Of course, simply saying that Jesus Christ is Lord and Saviour does not in itself make it true. Nor does saying that it could not be false make it true in our sense since that would make it true by definition. This would be so even if we did as a matter of fact—but for other reasons—believe that it was true without a shadow of doubt. On the contrary when the believer asserts that Jesus is Lord and Saviour he is asserting that something is the case and that certain conditions have

[1] John L. Austin, "Truth," in *Truth*, ed. George Pitcher, p. 23.

been met that justify his belief. That is to say, nothing in the statement itself can settle the issue of its truth unless, of course, he is willing to settle for a trivial truth. Clearly the assertion that Jesus Christ is Lord and Saviour is not a trivial truth even though it may be certainly true. Whatever certainty this truth possesses must be a certainty that is neither the certainty of commitment such as the existentialist wants nor the certainty of a mere tautology. If there is a certainty, it will be a certainty established by the fulfillment of certain conditions. The believer will want to say among other things that as *a matter of fact* Jesus Christ is Lord and Saviour. But the certainty of his belief is not the certainty of a definition or tautology. There *is* sufficient justification for his believing it, he will say. Could he be mistaken? Of course he could, in principle, just as I could be mistaken in believing that I am here writing this book. It is possible that I am only dreaming that I am writing it, but since the appropriate conditions have been met, I have good reasons for believing that I am here writing this book. Indeed it would be unreasonable if not irrational to doubt that I am.

The key to our claim upon truth is our assurance that certain specific and appropriate conditions have been met. This holds for any kind of true statement. Statements like "Jesus Christ is Lord and Saviour" or "God was in Christ" are true because certain conditions have been met, although it is for those who *know how to use* expressions such as these to say what these conditions are. Few believers will say that these statements are true simply because they happen to believe them or that they are true simply because they get a certain feeling from saying them. The conditions of truth are more demanding. This is why the "truth as encounter" or "truth as subjectivity" views are inadequate.

It is not my purpose here to stipulate these conditions. I can only inquire concerning what they are just as I may only inquire of the scientific community concerning the criteria for the truth of its statements. That believers do have conditions of belief and that these involve both what they say—doctrine, for example—and what they believe to be the case, as well as how they feel about the relationship, seems itself to be the case. Moreover the notion that truth can only be subjective is not only unduly pessimistic but arises from an inadequate analysis of the problem. Plato's argument against Protagoras can still be invoked against this kind of subjectivism. If truth is only what you or I happen to believe or want to believe, then the assertion that this is so is itself what you happen to believe and no more. What does hold generally is that "true" applies when specific conditions are met. But this is by no means to say that it is a purely linguistic matter.

But how do you know statements are really true when they *have* met your conditions? To the skeptic's question one can only counter with another question: How does anyone justify *any* truth? What does it mean to claim of any statement that it is true? The skeptic's problem is that he wants to put himself and everyone else in the position of saying that nobody could ever know that any statement were really true, and this would mean that we could not use the word "true" at all. But we *do* use it, and we use it meaningfully because we do not allow the skeptic to plague us with worries about whether it is really true whether the food we eat is really real or whether it is really true that the world really existed yesterday or other similar puzzlements. But why is it, we must ask, that we are irked by skepticism of this sort when it is applied to everyday material affairs but allow it to intimidate us when we speak of spiritual affairs?

And it does not help to argue that everyone must decide the truth for himself. This would be analogous to arguing that every scientist must have his own experiences or think his own thoughts and no one else's. But then whatever the scientist says is true would be true for him alone. From the fact that the conditions of biblical truth, for example, are not as universally agreed upon as the conditions for some other kinds of truth it does not follow that there are no conditions for biblical truth or that there is no such thing as biblical truth. The matter of authority is an internal one. How would a bank clerk, for example, go about authorizing the conditions for the truth of theoretical physics? It is for those who are making truth claims to identify the conditions that qualify what they say as truth. This is not subjectivism. It is objectivism—but not the sort that says either you claim truth by my rules—scientific or otherwise—or you do not claim it at all.

One kind of linguistic imperialism imagines that language must mirror a world of a certain kind thus binding us to one view of things and one view of words. Theology must avoid this kind of Babylonian captivity.

Yet simply to say that a true statement must say something that "corresponds to the facts" *could* be misleading. One might mistakenly think that because we use personal pronouns in connection with anything that God is or does, for example, that "correspondence to the facts" entails some kind of anthropomorphism. For example, suppose that when I say "God raised up Jesus" my words had to mirror facts somehow as though the words of themselves *could* mirror anything or as though they ever *do* mirror anything. Now I can say that God *literally* raised up Jesus, meaning that as a matter of fact God raised up Jesus, just as I might say that hydrogen *literally* combines with oxygen to form water, meaning that as a matter of fact hydrogen combines with oxygen to form water. In both cases the "truth" of the statements is a question of having a certain relationship of words and states of affairs that are determined by the kind and use of language involved and the rules appropriate to the language used. Thus it would be a mistake to assume that the literal truth of "God raised up Jesus" would *require* the visible activity of a shadowy figure, God, lifting the corpse of Jesus out of the tomb.

"There is no need," Austin argues—and correctly I believe—"for the words used in making a true statement to 'mirror' in any way, however indirect, any feature whatsoever of the situation or event; a statement no more needs, in order to be true, to reproduce the 'multiplicity,' say, or the 'structure' or 'form' of the reality, than a word needs to be echoic or writing pictographic. To suppose that it does, is to fall ... into the error of reading back into the world the features of language."[2] The issue is not one of reducing a language in use to a *more* intelligible one, but of learning how the language is used or how to use it so that it becomes intelligible.

A language is literally meaningless only if one is incapable of determining how it is used or of learning how to use it. To say, for example, that biblical language is meaningless as is often asserted today is to assume gratuitously that one cannot learn how it was used or how to use it. Moreover if being meaningful is one of the conditions of being true, and being meaningful is contingent on being used, we have only to ask if biblical language has been used in order to meet one of the conditions of truth.

We cannot claim superiority for certain kinds of language as vehicles of truth. Philosophical or scientific language has no inherent advantage over biblical language or the language of the believing and worshiping community. "The characteristics of a more developed language," Austin argued, "do not make statements in it any more capable of being true."[3] Demythologizing demands that we see the world through naturalistic eyes as though *this* would give us biblical truth. Even if the language of the New Testament were as mythical as Bultmann, for example, finds it to be, statements in New Testament language would be no less meaningful and capable of being true

[2] *Ibid.*, p. 24.
[3] *Ibid.*, p. 25.

than their demythologized substitutes. Indeed they would be more capable of being true on their own terms because they would be the appropriate way of saying what was being said.

One does not get at the truth of the New Testament by demythologizing it or finding an existential or secular meaning but by determining the conventions appropriate to its expression of truth. And this truth will not be solely the existential *kerygma* Bultmann seeks since he presupposes that *all* that the New Testament writers were doing was trying to express an existential truth. On the contrary it will be whatever it was they *did* say or *were* trying to do apprehended by the rules appropriate to *their* way of saying or doing it that will determine the truth they were uttering.

Part of the demand for a demythologized truth arises from the mistaken notion that to be literal a language must "mirror" the world. We experience difficulty, for example, imagining how God raised up Jesus because it is both unusual and unexplainable as a natural phenomenon. The existentialist says that the supernaturalism of the Bible is intolerable or incredible even though its language is really quite direct, concrete and intelligible on its own terms. Yet we tolerate the insuperably complex and abstract language of the scientific community. We do this, I believe, because we are willing to learn and to abide by the conventions of a scientific discourse which it would never occur to us to demythologize, but we refuse to take seriously the conventions of biblical supernaturalism. We are willing to play one language game but not the other; then we argue that our unwillingness is evidence for the nonexistence of what that language game deals with, and is justification for its reduction to some other language game.

Correspondence to fact by meeting specific conditions depends on rules that are agreed upon as appropriate to the kind of statement that is supposed to be true. To correspond will mean that certain conditions are met, and the conditions will be those imposed by the particular language in use, that is, by those who are using it. We may be tempted to say, "But what the believer says isn't really true," by which we will probably mean that *our* conditions for truth have not been met. And of course, if inapplicable conditions are imposed as the conditions of truth, we should not be surprised to discover that what we say is not true nor, for that matter, could be. We might say with the agnostic that we do not know whether the statement is true; but this will mean either that we do not know whether certain conditions are being met nor what those conditions should be, or, for that matter, what the statement may mean. I do not see that Christian statements are in principle different from statements of any other kind except that we tend to exaggerate their difficulties all out of justifiable proportion and to recommend radical reductionist programs that we would not dream of doing with other languages. Indeed we deliberately select *difficult* cases as our paradigms in order to encourage the notion that the meanings are never the obvious ones. Let us instead take a more obvious case.

In basketball it is true that a team makes a basket when certain conditions prescribed as part of the conventions of basketball have been met. The statement that team A scored two points is true if and only if certain conditions are met. For the statement that team A has scored two points to be true, that is, to "correspond to the facts," it is necessary that team A get the ball into the basket under the right conditions. Getting the ball into the basket and the other "right" conditions include among other things the consensus of the officials, and so on. It is absurd to say that the statement that team A scored two points is true because the statement itself—the words and structure—literally mirrors the event of scoring. It may be that in asserting the statement I have a mental image of what happened and by making the statement I am able to produce a similar image in the mind of another. But it is not even necessary that this image mirror the event.

Likewise my **confession** and the proposition that "Jesus Christ is Lord and Saviour" may be accompanied by an image of some sort in my mind that may or may not be shared by my hearer. But if what I say as part of what I do when I confess that Jesus Christ is Lord and Saviour is true, certain conditions will have been met which may or may not include any image I have in mind. Indeed it is doubtful that any particular image as such is a necessary condition in this instance although certain beliefs may be. We need to emancipate ourselves from the mirror model requirement. We need to see that statements are true so far as they relate words and the world in an appropriate way. When we are able to see that this applies to any kind of expression that purports to say something—even existential truth claims—we will not find theological truth claims as incongruous as they are supposed to be. "Even when a language does 'mirror' such features very closely (and does it ever?)," says Austin, "the truth of statements remains still a matter, as it was with the most rudimentary languages, of the words used being the ones conventionally appointed for situations of the type to which that referred to belongs. A picture, a copy, a replica, a photograph—these are *never* true in so far as they are reproductions . . . . a reproduction can be accurate or lifelike (true *to* the original) . . . . but only an (artificial) sign *for* something can be right or wrong."[4]

Language is a tool by which we get certain kinds of things done. Communication or *logos*—to use the suggestive Greek term—is something that happens. Action, we say, speaks louder than words. Why? Is it not because words alone may not be able to do the job required? Indeed not only need a statement not picture or mirror a state of affairs as such, it need not even be true, since *it may not be conveying information.* Austin notes that

recently it has come to be realized that many utter-

4 *Ibid.,* p. 25.

ances which have to be taken to be statements . . . are not in fact descriptive (of anything at all) nor susceptible (by any rules) of being true or false. When is a statement not a statement (in the sense of not being true or false)? When it is a formula in a calculus: when it is a performatory utterance; when it is a value-judgment; when it is a definition; when it is part of a work of fiction.[5]

What of the gospel, for example? Does it mirror some event like the making of a basket in basketball? Yet it *does inform.* It *does contain propositions.* It *does point to objective states of affairs.* Its truth is not simply existential—whatever that may mean. Yet no one would want to deny that some aspects of it are inexpressible. Who can express the wonder and the joy of His salvation? And it does a great deal more than inform. Yet again as a member of the community of believers, the believer has his reasons, his criteria, his standards and his conditions of belief. The fact that there is no complete agreement concerning what Christian believers want to say or that the difficulties of any full consensus may be insuperable is no grounds for contending either that there is no consensus at all or that there is no truth. The *difficulties* for establishing a truth cannot be taken as adverse evidence. From the fact that agreement may be lacking concerning ways to settle disputes, it does not follow that there can be no agreement, no settlement or no truth. If *these* were the conditions of truth and belief, most adults would not be married, would have starved to death, would have no education and probably no friends.

Of course there will be those who will simply reject biblical language on the grounds that it is the vehicle of superstition. For them there are no supernatural truths nor can there be. A basket will not count two points. Perhaps it will not count at all. Perhaps it does not even happen. Perhaps it is just a peculiar

[5] *Ibid.,* p. 29.

sort of way one feels when told that the team scored. But words like "true" and "truth" *are* used to refer to something other than feelings, and where they are existential instead of ordinary truths, they will be grounded nonetheless in facts.

There are then no naturally superior rules for establishing the relations between words and states of affairs such that one can say of one particular set that *that* and *only that* particular set may establish truth. To assert that there is, is to misunderstand the nature of language. God does not speak Hebrew or the language of science as such, but He *does* speak, and there are those who *do* hear. This is, I would suppose, what the discipline of hermeneutics is supposed to be about.

It is simply mistaken to assume that because the language of science, for example, is informative, propositional, and so on, the language of faith is not. Language is like a set of tools. It can do many things. It does not follow, for example, that because the language and conventions of truth in contemporary experimental science work with facts, biblical language does not. And it is sheer folly to suppose that the conventions for determining true statements about molecular structures or conditioned reflexes are those for determining whether God was in Christ.

We cannot suppose that the rules of one language like those of the natural sciences hold a monopoly on what can be said to be true in other languages. Nor can we suppose that truth is merely some kind of existential insight. We can and do link ourselves to objective reality in certain appropriate ways. As Christians, we respond to a God who reveals Himself to us. The who, what, when, where and why of this communication are determined in a manner appropriate to the nature of the communication itself. The God who communicates Himself in the person of Jesus the Christ and in the person of His Holy Spirit is the one and same God who communicates Himself in the written words of that Christ and in the written words of His disciples. Those words are as much the norm of

78

our faith as the Spirit Himself. They not only point to what our faith is all about, but they are the very words of that faith. To change them would not improve our faith. It would introduce another faith. Changing the rules does not improve the game. It introduces a new game.

But suppose we persist in wondering how we may know that *biblical* truth is truth. The answer, it seems to me, must be: How does one know that *any* truth is truth? How does one know that the world isn't an illusion? How does one know that George Washington isn't a mythical figure? How does one know that one's wife has not fallen out of love with him? One knows whatever is known—if anything is known—by means appropriate to what is known.

The believer knows that biblical truth is truth because the conditions of biblical truth have been met. This will be so even if we cannot agree fully as to what these conditions are. The Bible speaks to the believer's condition. He experiences what the Bible talks about. The eyes of faith reveal new things. His heart opens to new truth. His mind is transformed. He trusts the Bible, and the Bible speaks with his voice as well as the voice of God. Its authority is vindicated. Moreover he shares all this with other believers just as men everywhere share common distinctions between dreams and ordinary conscious experiences.

Of course, if I were to make the conditions of Christian truth the same as the conditions of scientific truth, if I were to try to verify peculiarly Christian claims in the manner that I verified beliefs about the weather, I shouldn't be surprised if I were to fail. Christian beliefs and beliefs about the weather are two different things. The manner appropriate to determining true beliefs about the weather is simply not the manner appropriate to determining true Christian beliefs. Yet so far as both can be known to be true in the manner appropriate to the truth claimed, they are the same. The fact that one may be more difficult to determine does not alter the fact that it is truth.

Christian truth is in principle no less immune to skepticism than is any truth. It is just that nonbelievers must justify their skepticism in a way they don't feel obliged to do in connection with other kinds of truth. If the biblical gospel is false, the skeptic must be sure that it is, since it is no trifling matter. He might miss on the weather and get a little wet. But if he misses on the gospel his destiny is threatened. Any philosopher knows that even apparently safe empirical truth claims can, if one wants to question them, be opened to all kinds of skeptical objections. It is just that it doesn't usually occur to most of us to get that worked up over beliefs concerning ordinary material objects and experience. There we can quite safely leave things as they are or as they appear to be. Yet on the matter of eternal life or the ultimate status of our existence, we not only become gravely concerned but we go out of our way to deny spiritual truths simply to justify our indifference or unbelief. The nonbeliever must persist in his skepticism. He can hardly afford not to. But the believer must also persist in his belief. He can hardly avoid doing so.

6

What About the
Existentialist's Bible?

THUS FAR I have tried to show that theology got into trouble when it rejected supernaturalism and propositional revelation and turned instead to existentialism. The reasoning of the theologian seemed to be something like this: The modern world view makes supernaturalism untenable. The Bible is so highly suspect for so many reasons that it can no longer serve as Christian authority. Existentialism seems to be both a viable way of approaching the theological problem and a way to keep alive the Christian faith. Existentialism gives us a kind of truth that is immune to the usual factual problems. We can rediscover what it means to speak of Christ without saddling ourselves with the beliefs of a discredited and outmoded book.

Professor Van Buren sums up the new view when he says that Christianity is about man, not about God. God is no more believable today than were the angels or demons to the scoffer of the recent past. For Van Buren, contemporary man must find in Jesus a fellow human being who was able to live above the meanness and despair of human existence and who gives us the hope that we can do the same. Van Buren's question is "How may a Christian who is himself a secular man understand the Gospel in a secular way?"[1] Put another way his question is "How may a Christian who is

[1] Paul M. Van Buren, *The Secular Meaning of the Gospel*, p. xiv.

an empiricist understand the Gospel in an empirical way?" For the existentialist the question is specifically "How may a contemporary Christian who can understand existentialism understand the gospel in an existential, nonpropositional way?" In either case the problem is How are we to understand the gospel today?

Let us take a typical example of what the Christian existentialist thinks about the gospel. This example, like that of Brunner earlier, is not the deliberate selection of a bad one in order to stack the cards of the argument. Quite the contrary. Brunner and my example below are examples of Christian existentialists in the best sense of the term. Par for the course would be the more openly nonbiblical existentialists who find little room for biblical concepts at all. Tillich, for example, starts his three-volume *Systematic Theology* with enthusiastic commitments to the Bible but soon finds any *actual* reference to it virtually unnecessary. And most Christian existentialists are inclined to hold that an overly generous use of Scripture is not *really* being biblical at all. They are not likely to be impressed by anyone who does make use of biblical authority of any sort. That is one reason why the Bible is sparingly used in this book. Biblically oriented existentialists like Brunner do depend on the Bible in a way that the more philosophically or culturally oriented existentialists like Tillich do not.

The current mood of Christian existentialism is well reflected in a typical statement appearing in the January, 1967, issue of the *Faculty Forum*. The feature essay is by Professor Leroy Troutner who is Assistant Professor of Education at the University of California at Davis. Troutner attempts to apply some of the insights of Kierkegaard to the understanding of Christian education. He nicely sums up the concern of the Christian existentialist:

Becoming a Christian ... involves not accepting a doctrine ... but grasping and holding fast to the eternal,

82

living Christ—the Teacher who as the sign of contradiction can speak only indirect to man. Christ does
not explain the basic tenets of Christianity for our
understanding. Rather as the Absolute Paradox, he
draws attention to himself in such a way as to reveal
the secret thought of the beholder. Christ as the sign
of contradiction forces man to choose.

When we ponder what Professor Troutner says in
the context of the truth as encounter problem, we note
the urgency of his desire to hold fast to the living
element of the encounter. We note also that his strategy is to avoid those elements that are the direct source
of the offense—supernatural belief—and to acknowledge instead that the scandal in Christian belief is
itself the *sine qua non* (absolute requirement) of
Christian faith. Yes, he says, the scandal is there, but
that is why you *can* believe in an existential way. All
those things you cannot believe are things you should
not believe because believing *in this way*, that is,
believing propositions, is not what becoming a Chris
tian is all about. Of course, the gospel does not make
ordinary factual sense, he argues. Statements like
John 3:16 are literal but not existential nonsense.
After all, Jesus Himself is the "Absolute Paradox."
Yet it is by virtue of *this* paradox that we are able to
gain existential self-understanding. It is by virtue of
what does not make sense, that is, the absurd, or what
offends, that we are forced to choose and make sense
of ourselves.

The Christian existentialist outflanks the unbeliever's rejection of the gospel. When the unbeliever says:
"The gospel does not make sense. The Bible is a
myth. The church is no longer relevant," and so on,
his existentialist sympathizer agrees with him. He
then goes on to explain that contrary to what is expected, the offense of faith is its great advantage
rather than disadvantage. Strange as it may seem, the
enemy of faith is really belief, not unbelief. He who
believes because he thinks he *does* understand Christ
in a propositional way crucifies Him anew. He' who

believes because he *does* understand God in a propositional way actually denies Him. He who *literally* believes the Bible rejects the Word of God! To understand or to believe in the ordinary sense is really to
misunderstand or disbelieve existentially. Faith is a
risk, not an assurance. It is possessed by commitment,
not knowledge. The believer must beware that his
belief does not distort his faith. His faith builds from
doubt rather than belief. Faith is "distorted by Biblical literalism," Tillich warns.[2] The existentialist
disarms both believer and unbeliever. Believers may
be men of no faith after all, while unbelievers may be
men of faith after all.

The existentialist enjoins us to be open to God *in
the present*. We are told that leaning on past revelation closes us to present revelation. But what if the
very thing we are not open to—the Scriptures themselves—*were* what God wanted us to be open to? Then
the very thing that we wanted to do—to be open to
God's Word—would be the very thing denied to us by
our gratuitous assumption that it was not His Word.

For the existentialist the Bible is like a private
medicine bottle to be used when needed. When the
bottle finally empties, he says, "God is dead. I must
now live without dependence on my medicine." All
along, of course, it was his own view of revelation and
truth, and his own low estimate of the Scriptures that
led him to his untimely conclusions. Having converted
the Scriptures into a private hunting preserve, he
hunted down the game until they were gone. His
strategy for saving the game fails for the reason that
the strategy is self-destructive.

If the new theology can find its way home, it will
not be by its own speculations. God will reappear to
reassert His authority and His Word. Indeed some of
the more perceptive of the new theologians make this
their key point. God is hidden, they say. He has
withdrawn Himself from our presence. He is temporar-

[2] Paul Tillich, *Dynamics of Faith*, p. 83.

ily unwilling to speak to us. But He *could* return, we are told. So far as this is included in the openness of the existentialist position, it is something to be applauded. God *is* the Lord of all. We *are* entirely in His hands. The believer knows this if he knows anything at all. To disavow it is to disavow the faith.

What the existentialist properly sees is that an open doctrineless existentialism which is *looking* for God is hardly worse than a smug belief which possesses yet possesses not. Nevertheless, it seems to me that it is better to be lost in lifeless belief than lost with no belief at all. Men have a way of being reawakened. But if there is no proclamation and no preacher, what hope is there? It is a fact that when the gospel is faithfully preached, however badly, results follow. The gospel may be too good to be true for many today, but it is never too good to be preached. And there will always be those who could not care less about it as well as those who find in it the key to eternal life.

The existentialist mistakes his own emotional response for the reality which provokes it. His problem is that having abandoned supernaturalism, he can no longer literally envisage the act of a gracious personal Being who is the Author of his salvation. He must restate the gospel in naturalistic terms as genuine self-understanding. Now of course it is absurd to speak of a supernatural work of grace as a natural occurrence. Yet this is what the existentialist appears to do. If supernaturalism must go, there is nothing left but to claim something amounting to supernatural grace despite the fact that there is no supernatural. Moreover to speak of the gospel as authentic self-understanding puts it in line for a reconciliation with the best religious and philosophical insight which uniformly claims this to be the goal of human existence.

Bultmann reassures us that there is help for us that is a *nonsupernatural* grace. But again, in view of its paradoxical nature, is it *less* unbelievable than the supernatural work of Christ? And the fact that a *man* Jesus did attain to the freedom of the new being is little comfort to the rest of us for whom it remains only a *possibility*. Even if the human Jesus really did actualize this possibility, I should not want to stake *my* salvation on the mere possibility of my doing the same. Life would be easier and more pleasant with the appropriate drugs and diversions. And this is exactly what many are concluding. It is only on the actuality and certainty of a supernatural event that the Christian can build his faith or hope. "How firm a foundation is Jesus Christ my Lord" are not idle words.

Medieval theologians and philosophers pictured God as the only Being whose existence is His essence. Even Descartes acknowledged the fundamental principle that only in God does existence precede essence—to use the existentialist's famous phrase. The existentialist would have us believe, however, that *man's* existence precedes his essence, that his "nothing" is made into "something." Man is what *he makes of himself*, they say. It is he who defines by his choices what it is to be human. He has nothing "going for him," the atheistic existentialists say. He does have a nonsupernatural grace, Christian existentialists like Bultmann say, and he also knows that the universal possibility of authentic existence was actualized in Christ. The paradigm man is Christ. He shows us what can be done, Bultmann argues. But on historical biblical and Christian grounds, the idea that man must or can "go it alone" is no less than original sin dressed up to look like salvation. If we protest to the existentialist that Christ did not understand Himself in the existentialist way, we are told that our conception of what He thought of Himself is really the early church's understanding of itself in the light of its proclamation of the gospel.

It is the loss of regard for the Bible and what it says that is the most important characteristic of the general retreat from theistic supernaturalism. This retreat aggravates all of the other difficulties that face theology. It is not simply a matter of trying to sustain a nostalgic regard for something that can no longer be taken

86

seriously, nor is it simply an unwillingness on the part of contemporary man to accept biblical authority. It is a question of not having any standard of Christian faith. If being Christian in any of the manifold senses of the term is a matter of what someone seriously stipulates it to be, so that anyone can propose a revision of the meaning, then Christianity can go in any direction that it happens to go and *that* direction—if the new theology is to have its way—will be the direction that revelation took it. This is the risk of faith, we are told. In the face of it, we are helpless to judge any pronouncement that is set before us. Indeed willingness to accept this predicament is the measure of our willingness to venture forth as men of faith, it is argued.

In the past Christians disagreed vigorously concerning the canons of their faith. Now there is no longer agreement that what the Bible says *counts* for what God says or that what the church says *counts* for what He says or, for that matter, could count for what He says. Today God can be made to say or to mean almost anything because it is the existentialist's encounter that determines what He says with an authority exceeding that of the Scriptures themselves. As we have seen, the encounter does in a significant sense take the place of God. The existentialists say that the Bible is to be used only if it fits our human purposes or if we can get around its difficulties. Any reference to "what the Bible says" per se or "thus saith the Lord" is regarded as naïveté or bombastic dogmatism. Is this attitude justified? I think not. For one thing the difficulties of the Bible are exaggerated out of all proportion with reason or the facts. Existentialists have traded on myths of their own making. For one thing, the whole demythologizing program is now in serious difficulty concerning the nature of its limits if there are any.

We need not deny that Jesus is the living Word in order to assert that the Bible is the written Word. And why is it the written Word? Several answers could be given. I shall argue here only that it is the written Word because its account was agreed upon by the first Christians as the account of what God said and did. If we cannot assign authority to the canonized version, to what *are* we to turn? If we cannot trust the authors of the canon, *whom* can or are we to trust? If *they* were mistaken, by what criteria are we to judge this? Either our witness is their witness and our beliefs theirs or we are not as they were, that is, Christians. This, it seems to me, is basic to the evangelical position.

According to the existentialists, the supernatural element in the Gospels and in primitive Christianity arose as the result of the mythopoeic activity of the early church as it reflected upon the Easter event which—according to them—is the transforming power of the gospel message. Yet interestingly Mascall notes that

the extreme scepticism about the [historical] reliability of their material which is manifested by many New Testament scholars does not seem to be supported by the small number of ancient historians who, having done their initial work in the non-biblical field, have later turned their attention to the origins of Christianity.[3]

What started as a general thesis that the Gospels had been corrupted *subsequent* to their writing, developed into the position that they were corrupted or at least shaped *in* the development and writing itself. It now seems to be the general view—if I understand it correctly—that the mythologizing that occurred was the natural inevitable and even desirable effect of the early church's effort to get its experience into the thought forms of the age. Thus we do not have today what Jesus actually said—to say nothing of what God said. Instead we have what the early church said about *its own experience* in terms of *its own understanding and needs*. What Jesus actually said or what is supposed

[3] Eric L. Mascall, *The Secularization of Christianity*, pp. 214-15.

to have actually happened or to have been revealed seems to become even more remote with every passing development of critical biblical scholarship. By the time the oral and written sources got cannonized, we are told, they were already pretty well doctored up.

We are now confronted, according to this view, with the task of reversing the process in order to uncover the existential root of the whole matter that gave rise to it in the first place. The reason given is that we simply cannot conceive of the original encounter in its own thought forms. Heidegger's *dasein* analysis is the most appropriate form by which to understand the encounter today, Bultmann believes. What is more, the early church made many serious mistakes as, for example, expecting the early return of Jesus. Thus the birth of Christianity was occasioned by errors compounded upon errors, and classical Christian belief is the result of many factors and outside influences, such as Greek philosophy, which are not part of the original *kerygma*. The only thing that is worthy of serious consideration is the existential *kerygma*, the truth of encounter, but only in its *present* rather than its original form. Thus the collapse of biblical authority and Christian belief today is accepted as a necessary occurrence since it signals the end of dogma and the emergence of an existential understanding of Christian faith.

But one wonders how the church could have emerged at all were the resurrection of Jesus not an historical event but some peculiar frenzy that seized His followers shortly after His death. Moreover from the fact that the natural world view of the New Testament is different from the natural world view today, we cannot conclude either that the New Testament writers deliberately or even inadvertently distorted their portrayal of events or that their understanding was necessarily mistaken. An ancient lover is not mistaken about his love simply because he does not know contemporary psychology. What God does is logically unrelated to any natural world view. The New Testament Greeks were as scandalized by the Christian claims as are any moderns, and could anyone say that Peter's everyday experience would make the resurrection of Christ any less surprising for him than for us?

The existentialist understanding of the Gospels encourages an unreasonable emphasis upon the interpretive activity of the early church. It is almost as if the early church entered into a conspiracy to create and distort the facts in order to suit its own needs. Citing Riesenfeld as his source, Professor Mascall notes that

> whatever else he was, our Lord was a Jewish rabbi . . . . His teaching would have been very largely given in stock rabbinic fashion to be learnt by heart and handed down by word of mouth . . . . One of the chief functions of the apostles was to watch over this tradition, which was regularly taught and passed on in the Church's gatherings for worship. It was this context of ordered instruction and not one of imaginative mythopoeia that was the *Sitz im Leben* of the transmission of the Gospel in the oral period.[4]

Robert M. Grant notes that "the evangelists regarded their function as that of bearing witness to Jesus Christ, not that of composing edifying fiction."[5] Careful memorization and, finally, careful commitment to writing much more nearly characterized the human side of events leading up to the production of the New Testament. We have been overly intimidated by the skepticism of the form critics who have exaggerated the unreliability of the Gospels as factual accounts.

The secular historian A. N. Sherwin-White writes that

> while Graeco-Roman historians have been growing in confidence, the twentieth-century study of Gospel narrative starting from no less promising material, has taken [a] gloomy turn in the development of form-

[4] *Ibid.*, p. 225.
[5] Robert M. Grant, *Historical Introduction to the New Testament*, p. 302.

criticism . . . . The divergences between the synoptic
gospels, or between them and the fourth gospel, are
no worse than the contradictions in the Tiberius material [of Tacitus].[6]

Again he notes "that those who had a passionate
interest in the story of Christ, even if their interest in
events was parabolical and didactive rather than historical, would not be led by that very fact to pervert
and utterly destroy the historical kernel of their material."[7] The point of all this is that secular historians
do not demand as much of their sources as do existentialist biblical scholars. Indeed the expectations of the
existentialist scholars would make a great deal of *any*
written history impossible.

What seems to be evident is that there is a persis-
tent bias against the supernatural. Whenever supernatural events are reported, the account is taken to be
interpretation or fabrication. Mascall's point is well
taken when he says that it is

> psychologically and theologically preposterous to sup-
> pose that, when the primitive Church found itself
> faced with some problem of belief or practice, it first
> of all made up its mind what it intended to do and
> then invented or garbled some utterance of Jesus in
> order to claim his support for its decision . . . . Still
> less does it seem to be probable that the material
> which is brought together in the Gospels is simply the
> upthrow of an outburst of mythopoeic frenzy result-
> ing from some mysterious and irrational "Easter-ex-
> perience" which attacked Jesus' disciples two days
> after his crucifixion and spread like a disease to those
> with whom they came into contact, so that the Church
> lost all sense of the distinction between fact and fic-
> tion.[8]

[6] Adrian N. Sherwin-White, *Roman Society and Roman Law in the
New Testament*, p. 187.
[7] *Ibid.*
[8] Mascall, p. 233.

The apostles and the early church were no more given to fantasies than are people of any age. Actually the New Testament writers appear to be keenly interested in getting the facts straight because of their utmost importance for the gospel message. It would seem that Paul's declaration in I Corinthians 15:3-7 or the opening words of the gospel according to Luke would indicate an explicit desire on their part to preserve with absolute fidelity the eyewitness accounts of the crucifixion and resurrection. "There is absolutely nothing to show that any of Jesus' teachings have been distorted or falsified," archaeologist W. F. Albright writes.[9]

So far as Christian existentialism is concerned, particularly as it is found in Tillich or Bultmann, the important thing is not that the historical events occurred as portrayed in the New Testament but that our understanding of ourselves is changed by the new insight we are able to get. As Macquarrie puts Bultmann's position, the minimum of factual truth needed is "simply that there was someone who once exhibited in history the possibility of existence which the *kerygma* proclaims."[10]

But if the New Testament is what Bultmann believes it to be, then how does *he* know of any gracious saving act of God or for that matter of any Jesus who exemplifies it? It would seem that he could no more know this than he knows or does not know that there was a Jesus at all. And why is not the *kerygma* itself mythological as Buri properly noted? How can we abstract the existential from the factual and make it stand on its own? I believe we cannot do so. The two stand or fall together.

Despite Bultmann's protest, if we follow the road that existentialism takes us, we arrive at a fully dekerygmatized as well as demythologized gospel that is

[9] W. F. Albright, in W. D. Davies and D. Daube (eds.), *The Background of the New Testament and Its Eschatology*, p. 171.
[10] Macquarrie, p. 93.

no more than a philosophy of existence. Jesus Christ becomes just another one of the numerous archetypal redeemer symbols that inhabit human unconsciousness and periodically emerge into consciousness only to resubmerge after a time. This is, of course, exactly what the radical theologians have concluded, that the New Testament God in Christ has disappeared from contemporary consciousness.

Existentialism neither gives rise to nor preserves Christian faith. Its effort to dissociate faith from history fails either to discredit the factual plausibility of the Scriptures or to liberate the *kerygma* from its historical limitations. Nor can existentialism preserve the faith with its doctrine of truth as encounter, for faith must be grounded in facts which are believed. To compromise the objective reality of God or His salvation only accommodates Christian faith to unbelief. It does not nurture faith. The existentialist fails to provide a new understanding of God or truth. Instead he gives us a rootless faith that withers before our eyes. With existentialism, "no longer is it possible to speak of a Biblical faith or a Biblical religion or even of a distinct and singular Biblical God," Altizer correctly contends.[11] On this point radicals and Evangelicals can agree. Only the existential occupants of a halfway position cannot.

11 Thomas J. J. Altizer, *The Gospel of Christian Atheism,* p. 89.

7

Is There a Religionless
Christianity?

IT IS NOT UNCOMMON for the Christian existentialist
to think of himself as a "religionless" Christian partly
because he has rejected supernaturalism and partly
because he has abandoned the doctrinal and institu-
tionalized forms of the faith. The "religionless" Christian takes his cue from Barth's significant utterance
that "in religion man bolts and bars himself against
revelation by providing a substitute, by taking away
in advance the very thing which has to be given by
God."[1] He then concludes with Bonhoeffer that religion is incompatible with true Christianity and that
"he must therefore plunge himself into the life of a
godless world, without attempting to gloss over its
ungodliness with a veneer of religion or trying to
transfigure it."[2]

Now Christianity, however understood or misunderstood, has indeed posed obstacles to God's will for
man, and orthodoxy should be reminded of its need to
repent of its idolatries and of its distortions of the
gospel. Religion—and particularly organized religion
—has been on occasion the gospel's greatest enemy. No
sincere Christian is justified in believing that he or his
church is free from fault. He should stand ready to be
chastened by Barth or Bonhoeffer or anyone else for

[1] Karl Barth, *Church Dogmatics, I: The Doctrine of the Word of God,*
Part 2, p. 303.
[2] Dietrich Bonhoeffer, *Letters and Papers from Prison,* p. 222.

having allowed the love of God that was in Christ to go out of his life and the life of his church.

But the "religionless" Christian does not just remind orthodox believers of this. He lays claim to a new revelation that nowhere says exactly what Christianity should mean, or could mean, or how a church or belief open to the new revelation could properly be called Christian at all. How could we know, asks Leon Morris, "whether this is in line with the mind of Christ, or whether it is another form of man's perennial self-sufficiency?"[3] One could hardly call upon the Holy Spirit to bear witness on behalf of the new religionless revelation since the Spirit's witness is no part of religionless Christianity—certainly not as a *supernatural* aid.

Christians are not orthodox and evangelical simply because they are unable or unwilling to give up old ideas. They are orthodox and evangelical because that is what being Christian means to them. It is one thing for the new religionless Christian to remind the "old" evangelical Christian of his moral and spiritual shortcomings, such as his failure to make his convictions relevant to the world or his reluctance to be open to new understanding of God's Word. Indeed, the sincere Evangelical is painfully aware of his failures. But to urge upon him the notion that Christianity is *really* religionless is simply to engage in a persuasive redefinition of a familiar term and attempt to keep for special purposes the desirable emotive force of the term Christian.

Religion can be *made* objectionable by definition. This is what Bonhoeffer does when he defines it as that activity which is isolated from everyday life, morbidly personal, and prone to believe in a God who runs to our aid at our beck and call. Few Evangelicals ever really saw it in just *that* way. And because some people are mistaken about their religion, it does not follow that what they are mistaken about is itself objectionable or an obstacle to truth, even though their

[3] Leon Morris, *The Abolition of Religion*, p. 29.

mistaken beliefs and behavior most certainly are both.

The problem, we are told, is that men have separated the sacred from everyday life in a way that has distorted and impoverished that life. The answer, however, is not abandonment of necessary logical distinctions like "sacred" or "secular." It is to acknowledge the idolatrous tendency by disengaging the two and sincerely trying to cope with it. Nothing can be gained from confusing distinctions that must be made in order to *speak* of our lives and of the conduct of those lives.

The Evangelical does not seek to escape from the common life as the religionless Christian accuses him of doing. He seeks rather to transform it in the only way he knows how. On the contrary it is the religionless Christian who is seeking to escape from the religious part of life. He wants to find God in *all* of life by *not* finding Him in the religious part of it. He wants to identify the sacred with the secular not in order to sacralize the latter but to secularize the former. But abandonment of the church, of personal piety, and even of personal salvation happens to be the abandonment of the very substance of the beliefs and practices of most Christians past and present. We must ask, Is *their* religion so defiled that nothing short of seeking God in the streets and slums will do? Religionless Christianity identifies openness to the Holy Spirit with abandonment of that very Spirit. It identifies acceptance of the world with acquiescence to it. "God is teaching us," Bonhoeffer says, "that we must live as men who can get along very well without him."[4]

Strangely, religionless Christianity argues that it is not the secular man come of age who obstructs God's new revelation but the pietistic evangelical believer. But how is it, we ask, that biblical doctrine should be so interpreted that the man who openly denies his need of God turns out to be God's own instrument of revelation, while the man who acknowledges God as

[4] Bonhoeffer, p. 219.

96

the Author of that which God is supposed to be doing through the nonbeliever, turns out to be the chief obstacle? The Bible clearly shows that God uses those who are not His obedient servants, as well as those who are. Perhaps the Evangelical needs to be reminded of his pride and waywardness, though of all people he is the most likely to be aware of it. Indeed it is his critic who finds him to be *neurotically* aware of it. He finds the Evangelical clinging to the God of the past, a God who, in Bonhoeffer's words, needs to be "edged out of the world" so that men can "live a 'worldly' life and so participate in the sufferings of God at the hands of a godless world."[5]

Religionless Christianity holds not only that evangelical Christianity is no longer relevant but also that it *can* no longer be relevant. But even if it were true that evangelical Christianity *is* irrelevant, it does not follow that it is necessarily so. From the fact that some Evangelicals may no longer be the instruments of God's will, it cannot be concluded that evangelical Christianity as a whole is not or *could not* be the instrument of God's will. Historically, evangelical Christians have led the way in most of the great movements of the Spirit of God, including important social reforms, and it is by no means true that the new Christian holds a monopoly of social concern. Indeed, his general theological confusion lessens his effectiveness as a reformer, and his political involvements may seriously overshadow his influence for good because he may mistake his own fallible convictions about the resolution of difficult social problems for a revelatory absolute of some sort.

One suspects that the non-Evangelical would like to shed old-fashioned evangelical responsibility for personal evangelism but nonetheless preserve the appearance of as much biblical justification for his position as he can muster. Bonhoeffer makes this clear when he asks: "Is it not true to say that individualistic concern for personal salvation has almost completely left us

[5] *Ibid.*, pp. 219, 222.

all?" He then goes on to ask reassuringly: "Is [this] not, at bottom, even biblical? Is there any concern in the Old Testament about saving one's soul at all? Is not righteousness and the kingdom of God on earth the focus of everything, and is not Romans 3:14ff., too, the culmination of the view that in God alone is righteousness, and not in an individualistic doctrine of salvation?"[6] But on the very next page he makes the revealing statement that he is "thinking over the problem at present how we may *reinterpret* in the manner 'of the world'—in the sense of the Old Testament and of John 1:14—the concepts of repentance, faith, justification, rebirth, sanctification and so on."[7]

Of course, all this is just one secular theologian's ambiguous position and one that was set forth over twenty years ago. Yet what Bonhoeffer wrote under the understandable stresses of life in a Nazi prison has become the rallying cry for a wholesale defection from New Testament beliefs. Where familiar terms or concepts are retained they are retained in unrecognizable form and mostly by the very same people who hold that it was the early church that cast the *kerygma* in the distorted patterns of their thought! The religionless Christian wishes to abolish religion, by which he means more specifically evangelical Christianity in virtually all of its most familiar expressions—the church, personal piety, holy living, evangelism and substantive Bible beliefs.

One of the weapons in the arsenal of secular Christianity is its claim that evangelical Christianity is both fragmented in its witness and demented in its other-worldliness. This weapon turns out, however, to be a kind of Freudianlike projection, because those who believe that religionless or secular Christianity is a unified witness or that its ideas are firmly attached to this word are victims of their own wishful thinking. Bishop Robinson takes the liberty of lumping Bonhoeffer, Bultmann and Tillich together in the same paragraph

[6] *Ibid.*, p. 168.
[7] *Ibid.*, italics supplied.

for obviously strategic reasons, but however unified these thinkers may be in their rejection of evangelical orthodoxy and supernaturalism, they are poles apart in their estimate of "religion." For Tillich, contemporary man is still very much the *homo religiosus* he has always been. He has not come of age so far as he can be said to no longer need God. Bonhoeffer on the other hand says that "the Christian is not a *homo religiosus*."[8] "Tillich," he says, "set out to interpret the evolution of the world . . . in a religious sense . . . but it felt entirely misunderstood, and rejected the interpretation."[9] Is Bonhoeffer with Bultmann's Christian existentialism? Hardly. Bultmann, he says, "goes off into a typical liberal reduction process."[10] Nor is there agreement between Bultmann and Tillich, for whom "demythologizing" is only "remythologizing."

Religionless Christianity capitalizes on the current dislike of religion of any kind by saying that secular or existential Christianity is not a religious Christianity. The process is verbal rather than substantive. It does not allow religion in some new sense to replace religion in the old sense unless, of course, religionless Christianity is religion in this new sense—in which case it turns out to be religion after all.

The situation is something like this. If being religious, and particularly being Christian, is culturally approved, then it will be appropriate for good people to be religious, and religious in a Christian way. If it is Christianity that is out of vogue but being religious that is not, then it will be the thing to be religious in an "open-minded," nonchristian sort of way, recognizing the great truth that after all it is being religious that really counts, and not being Christian, since all religion is at bottom the expression of the same virtue. But if *all* religion is viewed as bad or out of date or irrelevant, then *any* form of it, including Christianity, is likely to be viewed as undesirable. Hence the strate-

---

[8] *Ibid.*, p. 225.
[9] *Ibid.*, p. 198.
[10] *Ibid.*, p. 199.

gy is to say: "We are Christians, but we are not religious Christians," or better yet, "We are 'existential' rather than 'religious' or 'supernatural' Christians" since existentialism is "in" while religion or supernaturalism is not.

The "new" truth is that Christianity is not supposed to be supernatural or religious, at least not when it comes of age. The existentialist says further that it was never, as a matter of fact, more than existential. Hence to be Christian is really to be *secular* in the best sense of the term. *This*, we are told, is what people really wanted all along—that is, to be unfettered by otherworldly religion, salvation myths or even moral law. And *this* is what God has wanted for us all along, too, so far as we can meaningfully speak of God wanting anything at all. So far as the hosts of Christian saints past and present witness differently, they are mistaken. Now we can really live in and for *this* world with the full assurance that our former yearning for righteousness and the life to come was a premature and neurotic effort to avoid the common life of this world.

Of course, it will be argued that all Bonhoeffer meant was that we must learn to live so as not to expect God to intervene on our behalf whenever we ask Him to. Yet if Bonhoeffer has anything to say that has not already been said by historical orthodoxy, it is that God in the old sense has no part of life in the new sense. Indeed, that is the way we must understand him when he says: "Now that it has come of age, the world is more godless, and perhaps it is for that very reason nearer to God (in the new sense) than ever before."[11]

But we find ourselves asking questions like these: Why should the term Christian be kept at all? Is there some desirable emotive force in it that the "new" Christian wants to retain? How, for example, did one learn to use a term like Christian? Are we not referred to clear-cut examples of Christians that non-Christians

[11] *Ibid.*, p. 124.

100

as well as Christians—including Bonhoeffer—would accept as paradigms of the use of the term? And where are these to be found? Are they not to be found in the lives and deaths of the loyal followers of Christ? Surely the apostles themselves ought to qualify, and what did *they* think Christianity was all about? What is *their* witness in the New Testament? And if they do not qualify, who can? Bonhoeffer? But why not Hudson Taylor or Charles Spurgeon?

With arguments remarkably similar to those advanced today, the early Gnostics tried to make the Christian gospel more intelligible and intellectually satisfying to those who sought philosophical props for their faith. Christian writers did too, but their primary concern was the gospel per se and not accommodation or reinterpretation. Laeuchli calls attention to the fact that the term *Pater* (Father) occurs over four hundred times in the New Testament. He stresses that language about "God the Father" is one of the distinctive marks of Christian language as contrasted with Gnostic.[12] Gnosticism, as he clearly shows, finds it necessary to reinterpret the ideas of God. "Father" satisfies the Gnostic no more than it does the religionless Christian existentialist today as "the ultimate designation for the Christian God; he is in reality a deity above fatherhood ... the God beyond."[13] What the religionless Christian winds up saying is that God is a "depth," "beyond," "ground" or "presence" as if *these* were persons or whatever it is that does what persons do.

But the Christian's God is not *just* a "ground of being" and so on—whatever these may mean. He is the divine Person, the New Testament God the Father, who speaks in all of life, but in a supernatural spiritual way, and who reveals the mind of Christ in those who have invited Him into their hearts and lives. What the Evangelical says is that God in *this* sense should be in all of life, *including* the religious part of it as well. If God is to transform all of life, He

[12] Samuel Laeuchli, *The Language of Faith*, p. 33.
[13] *Ibid.*, p. 34.

101

must also transform the religious part of it. This is quite different from saying that there is no sacred part of life or that the divine is only a transcendent feature of the secular.

The problem is not one of existentializing the religious understanding of men who have not yet come of age but of getting God into that very religious understanding and transforming it so that it is no longer all of the things that make the religionless Christian want so badly to get rid of it. And here is where the Evangelical can concur with Tillich's belief that man is in desperate need of overcoming his estrangement from God and his fellowman. But that overcoming will be a supernatural gift of grace enacted by an indwelling supernatural spirit which alone can overcome the forces of this life. It is not merely the existentialist's "new being" or "self-understanding" or the experience of some "presence."

8

What About the Analytical Alternative to Existentialism?

IT IS NOT UNCOMMON to encounter the idea that philosophy threatens only evangelical Christian belief. Indeed, if the new secular Christian were to have his way, he would have us believe that he alone and not the orthodox believer had the support of all recent developments in philosophy. "The application of the methods of modern philosophy to the problems of modern theology has been barely begun," writes Professor Van Buren. These methods, he believes, will produce an "analysis of the language of the New Testament, the Fathers, and contemporary believers [which] will reveal *the secular meaning of the Gospel*."[1]

Certainly it would be a mistake for any Christian to believe that analytical or linguistic philosophy is wholly incompatible with believing Christianity or that Van Buren's secular theology is a necessary conclusion of philosophical analysis. Indeed Van Buren arrives at his "no-God" conclusions by a use of linguistic philosophy that is neither correctly understood nor correctly applied. Actually the new secular theology has as many philosophical difficulties as the views it seeks to replace. Evangelicals, however, are often intimidated by their opponents' claims as well as

[1] Paul M. Van Buren, *The Secular Meaning of the Gospel*, pp. 104, 19, italics supplied.

by their own mistaken notion that philosophy per se is the believer's nemesis.

Philosophical method, as it is generally understood today, is essentially neutral, even though some of its practitioners certainly are not. It need not be captivated by any particular picture of the way things are—such as, for example, the positivist picture of a world in which meaningful language exactly mirrors physical facts and physical facts only. Not all scientists are captivated by this positivist picture. Nor are most philosophers. Yet some theologians have apparently fallen under its spell, and Professor Van Buren, for example, tries to build a secular theology upon its dogma of meaning by verification alone.

Most philosophical analysts today would want to say that the criterion of empirical verifiability is limited to the identification of meaningful empirical statements. Yet Van Buren insists that "the heart of the method of linguistic analysis lies in the [explusive] use of the verification principle."[2] Despite his verbal rejection of the older form of analytical philosophy known as logical positivism, he nonetheless remains a prisoner of its picture of the way language relates to the world. What Van Buren wants is an empirical Christianity that will not offend what he takes to be the contemporary empirical mind. What he presents us, however, is neither empirical as the philosopher would see it nor Christian as the believer would see it.

The truth claims pictured in New Testament language are no less true than those pictured in the demythologized and empirical language Van Buren wants. The "new" statements that Van Buren claims give "the secular meaning of the Gospel" are no more capable of "mirroring the facts"—that is, of being true on *his own terms*—than are the original statements. Indeed, they are less capable of being true on any terms, if only because they are not in terms "conventionally appointed," as analyst Austin would put it,

[2] *Ibid.*, p. 104.

"for the situation of the type to which that referred to belongs."[3]

"The problem of the Gospel in a secular age," argues Van Buren, "is a problem of the logic of its apparently meaningless language."[4] To make the language of the Gospel meaningful, he proposes—to use Professor Mascall's description—to "substitute a statement which is [empirically] meaningful for one which is [apparently] meaningless under cover of expressing the *true* meaning of the [otherwise] meaningless statement."[5]

In other words, Van Buren proposes to translate all supernatural or otherwise "meaningless" statements of the Christian into verifiable and therefore meaningful statements. These will give us, he believes, the *secular* or *nonsupernatural* meaning of the gospel. Thus when the New Testament writers speak of Jesus as the Son of God, they are, according to Van Buren, saying the most that they can say about any *man* empirically; verification comes in at the point where one can describe behavior or other observable phenomena. For example, to confess Jesus Christ as the Son of God is, according to Van Buren, to announce an intention to live the way of life exemplified by Jesus. Thus the issue of the meaning of such words as "God," "Son of God," and so on, is resolved by their reduction to what Van Buren believes to be their equivalent *secular* terms.

Summed up, Van Buren is saying—to use his own words—that "unless or until a theological statement can be submitted in some way to verification, it cannot be said to have a meaning in our language game."[6] By "verification," however, he does not mean what is in fact taken by believers themselves to be verification of their claims in a spiritually appropriate sense. He means verification according to the "modified verifica-

[3] John L. Austin, "Truth," in *Truth*, ed. George Pitcher, p. 25.

[4] *Ibid.*, p. 84.

[5] Eric L. Mascall, *The Secularization of Christianity*, p. 93.

[6] Van Buren, p. 105.

tion principle," that is, verification as defined by his positivist philosophical picture. By "our language game" he means, not the way in which the Christian community does in fact use Christian language, but the way *he* does in fact use Christian language, that is, the way *he* is going to use it according to his positivist picture. Thus he is not even as close to being orthodox as the existentialist since the latter *does* speak of the "mighty acts of God" or a *kerygma*, however much he may have reinterpreted them. Not even this will do for Van Buren since nothing short of a complete translation of biblical into empirical terms will satisfy him.

Now most linguistic philosophers hold that language *may* be used to give empirical information, including information about one's future behavior, but it need not do so to be meaningful. They believe that one must note exactly what is being done with language in terms of its own logic. The rules of football cannot make sense of basketball even though these activities may bear some similarity to each other. Nor can the rules of physics and the language appropriate to it make sense of praying. Perhaps only those who play basketball or pray can make sense of what they are doing, but this does not appear to be the case. Some people can do both, and many other things as well. One can learn to do these things just as one can become converted and make as his own the witness of the New Testament.

We need not suppose that we cannot make sense of what the first Christians were doing, for example, since we can learn to do what they were doing by sharing their witness. Whatever the Christian believer is doing when he uses the language of the believing community, it is his activity. The philosopher's explanation of it is something else. The analyst's question is not "How can I translate what the believer is doing into terms that will be acceptable to those who are playing my language game?" as Van Buren wants. It is simply "What is the Christian believer doing?" There is no *secular* meaning of the gospel; there is only *the gospel*.

If giving information happens to be a part of what is being done, truth then becomes an issue. But the question of truth is distinct from the question of meaning. Even if what the Christians were saying were not true—and there is no logical necessity for this—it is meaningful on its own terms if it is doing its job. That is, it makes sense even though it does not happen to be true. I have already said a few things about the problem of truth in an earlier chapter of this book.

The analyst cannot by himself settle the question of truth; he can only note inconsistencies and other irregularities. Truth is not solely internal to what is said. Nor can the analyst force-fit language *in use* into his own particular picture of the way things are. He may not, as does Van Buren, reduce statements using the word "God" into statements about behavior or anything else on the ground that the word is meaningless by the rules of *his* language game. He may "rearrange" language in order to clarify what is going on or try different pictures in an effort to find the most appropriate or instructive one. But he cannot effect a straightforward reduction. Even if the believer were "bewitched"—to use Wittgenstein's well-known term— by his supernatural picture of things, as Van Buren thinks he is, this would not justify the substitution by Van Buren of his own "bewitchment" by the positivist picture of things for the believer's supernatural picture of things. And what I have said here of Van Buren applies with equal force to all existentialist theologians who attempt reductions, revisions or "improvements" of the believer's language.

What counts for the New Testament believer is what the New Testament writers themselves were doing when they used the terms "God" and "Father"—not what Van Buren does in his language game. "I'm trying," he says, "to understand the Bible on a naturalistic or humanistic level. . . . Its language about God is one way—a dated way among a number of ways—of saying what it is Christianity wants to say

107

about man and human life and human history."[7] But to use linguistic analysis as Van Buren says he is doing would be to understand the language of the New Testament on its own *supernaturalistic* terms, not on Van Buren's naturalistic terms.

Of course we *could* take "meaningful" to denote what Van Buren wants; but that would not make the believer's use of "God" any less meaningful by his own rules. As a matter of fact, it would not make the nonbeliever's use any less meaningful if he used the word "God" in its conventional way. As evidence of the meaninglessness of the term "God," Van Buren points to the fact that there are those who no longer use the term. But there have always been those who were unable to use the term "God" as *Christians use it* or who were, for that matter, unable to use it at all. What has not always been true, he thinks, is that believers themselves no longer use the term "God" in a supernaturalistic way. That, however, is an empirical question to be settled not by philosophical speculation or prescription but by looking at the facts.

The facts are that there *are* many people who do know how to use the term "God" and for whom it is therefore meaningful. To persist as Van Buren does in pointing to those who do not know how to use it and for whom it is meaningless is to persist in mistaking a tautology for an informative truth. That those who no longer know how to use the term "God" find it meaningless is necessarily true in the same sense that it is true that those cats that are no longer black are no longer black. But the substantive question is whether there are any black cats. This is something that Van Buren ought to consider but does not. Instead he makes a logiclay odd use of the term "believer" to include those who no longer find the term "God" meaningful in a supernatural way. Indeed, one could say that this is the substance of his whole concern:

[7] Reported by Ved Mehta in the *New Yorker* (Nov. 13, 1965), pp. 148, 153.

"How can the Christian who is himself a secular man understand his faith in a secular way?"[8]

Unlike Bishop Robinson who tries to secularize the gospel for the sake of the outsider, Van Buren tries to secularize it for the sake of the insider for whom the supernatural God of the New Testament is no longer believable. But clearly when Van Buren refers to *these* "insiders" as "Christians" and "believers" he is using language in a way that is unconventional if not downright persuasively deceptive and misleading.

If the language of the New Testament is dated, as Van Buren says, then he must admit that the New Testament writers did use "God" in a "dated way" to refer to a supernatural Being. But if *this* is true, how can he *also* say that when they spoke of Jesus as the Son of God, they were only paying Him compliments as an exceptional man whose way of life they were inspired to emulate? The New Testament writers did not have to put "God" in quotation marks to note an odd or unempirical use of the term. The rules of their language game were such that the term "God" was used among other things to refer to a supernatural Being who is real in the same sense—though not in the same way—that anything is real. Moreover, they obviously intended to be informative about what God did, as, for example, in the opening passages of Luke's gospel.

Van Buren's suggestion that the New Testament writers were doctoring up their accounts of Jesus in order to point up His enormous influence on their lives is implausible. "To suggest," as Mascall writes, "that the primitive church deliberately embroidered the simple human life of Jesus with a mass of mythical and largely miraculous material in order to convince either itself or outsiders of the authenticity of a purely psychological 'Easter experience' is to attribute to the first generation of Christians a degree of conscious sophistication for which there is really no evidence."[9]

[8] Van Buren, p. 2.
[9] Eric L. Mascall, *The Secularization of Christianity*, p. 74.

Moreover, if the New Testament accounts *are* as factually suspect as Van Buren and the existential biblical scholars claim, it would indeed require a blind leap of faith to justify anything that Van Buren wants to believe about the historicity of Jesus' life and death and the historicity of the event of the "Easter experience" as well. I do not see that what orthodoxy says is any less empirical on Van Buren's own grounds than what *he* says when he writes that "in saying that God raised up Jesus, the disciples indicated that what had happened to them was fundamental to their life and thought."[10] Yet this is what he wants to identify as a secular meaning of the gospel that is at once empirical and Christian. He seems to say to us that we ought to live as though there were a God even though we know there is not and even though we do not have any idea what it means to believe that there is not.

Why, we ask, is the term "God" so much of a problem for Van Buren? Why is he obliged to arrive at a no-God conclusion? And why is this conclusion mistaken and unnecessary?

The term "God" is a problem for him because he does not know, he says, exactly what it is that he is supposed to be talking about when he uses it. In the positivist picture, a term is meaningless unless it can be used to denote something in an empirical way. When statements appear to speak of Jesus' belief in God, for example, they are—according to Van Buren— really statements about Jesus' relationship to other persons—His freedom to be a man among men, a man for other—to use the Bonhoeffer phrase—and so on. "Today, we cannot even understand the Nietzschean cry that 'God is dead!'" says Van Buren, "for if it were so, how could we know? No, the problem is that the *word* 'God' is dead."[11] Yet Van Buren does not want to say that the terms "God" and "Father" were meaningless for Jesus, since Jesus certainly did use

[10] Van Buren, p. 133.
[11] *Ibid.*, p. 103.

110

them. Perhaps a verifiable or secular meaning or use can be identified that will restore their meaningfulness today. This is the task Van Buren sets for himself.

Van Buren can be read to say that there is *literally* no God, however, that is, no supernatural personal God in the conventional biblical and theistic sense of the term. He can be taken as an atheist in this sense. But whether there really is a God in this sense is not his main point. His main point is that the term "God" is meaningless, so that empirically speaking it is pointless to ask whether there is a God:

> The empiricist in us finds the heart of the difficult not in what is said about God, but in the very talking about God at all. We do not know "what" God is, and we cannot understand how the "word" God is being used. It seems to function as a name, yet theologians tell us that we cannot use it as we do other names, to refer to something quite specific.[12]

Here Van Buren's captivity to the positivist picture of language and the world leads him to adopt a theory of meaning which holds that for an expression such as "God" to have a meaning is for it to refer to or name "something quite specific" like "Fido." This theory of meaning has been generally abandoned by the very linguistic philosophy which Van Buren says he is using and by most of the linguistic philosophers whose views he says he shares. It is "this view of the meaning of words," notes Professor Hall, that "seems to underlie Van Buren's inability to accept the meaningfulness of the term or name 'God', and ultimately to opt for a 'secular' Christology (as he understands it) rather than a theology."[13]

But the philosopher Wittgenstein, to whom Van Buren refers as "fundamental to ... [his] whole study," perhaps did more than any other philosopher

[12] *Ibid.*, p. 84.
[13] Robert Hall, "Theology and Analysis," *The Christian Scholar* (Winter, 1965), p. 309.

to expose the errors of the theory of meaning presupposed by Van Buren. Later, Austin showed that one could make true statements about objective facts without having, as Van Buren thinks, to keep the theory of meaning that makes terms like "God" meaningless. In other words, "Van Buren has based his whole case for the meaninglessness of the term 'God' on the conclusions of a movement which, for the most part, has long since been laid to rest."[14]

The doctrine that Van Buren mistakenly believes to be the current doctrine is the doctrine that every meaningful expression must have a referent. But there are many meaningful words (that is, words that are capable of being used) that do not "refer to something quite specific," do not have a referent—words like "if," "because," "induction," and so on. The word "God" would be meaningful even if Van Buren's atheism happened to be true! Van Buren virtually acknowledges this by trying to identify its *naturalistic* instead of supernaturalistic meaning. In other words, because he thinks the ordinary and New Testament use of "God" to refer to a supernatural Being is empirically meaningless, he tries to reinstate its meaningfulness by finding a secular use or meaning and developing a secular theology.

But the strategy is unnecessary because it is occasioned by a faulty theory of meaning. Van Buren cannot support his claim for a secular or no-God theology on the grounds that *analysis* shows that such a theology is necessary in order to make sense of the word "God." The word "God" already makes sense on grounds independent of any "secular" or "empirical" use such as Van Buren wants or thinks it needs. It is simply not necessary to identify the meaning of a word as it is actually used in its context with "the use of the verification principle," as Van Buren wants to do. Hence the term "God" need not have a secular meaning

[14] J. H. Gill, "A Case of Mistaken Identity," *The Christian Scholar* (Summer, 1966), p. 149.

or use in order to be meaningful, and Van Buren's whole effort to save the gospel by secularizing it is both unnecessary and misconceived.

What is at stake is not the believer's claims about God and the gospel but Van Buren's claim that they must be cast in secular terms. Perhaps Van Buren *does* use terms like "God" or "Gospel" in a secular way. But it is not necessary that they be used in his secular and unconventional way in order for them to be meaningful. According to him, when the Christian follows the example of Jesus by praying, "Our Father which art in heaven . . . ," it is meaningless to say that he is addressing a supernatural Being. We have to say that he is expressing an intention to live the way of life exemplified by Jesus if we are to make "secular" sense. No doubt part of what the Christian does when he prays in this manner is to declare his intention to follow the example of Jesus; but clearly his use of "God" and "Father" is not confined to that.

Since the term "God" has no referent and events unexplainable by natural laws cannot occur, whatever is said that involves either of these must be translated into what Van Buren believes the New Testament writers meant in a secular or empirical way. The Apostle Paul, then, did not really mean that God raised up Jesus; he meant that he, Paul, got a new slant on life.

But how does Van Buren know this? By his own positivist criteria, the statement of his about what Paul was doing when he wrote of God raising up Jesus is either empirically informative or analytically necessary. That is, Van Buren's reduction of God-statements to psychological or behavior descriptions is either true by verification or true by definition. But it is hardly true by definition, since it would then only represent Van Buren's proposal to interpret Paul in this unconventional way or define his terms in a certain way. And we are interested in what the apostle was actually doing when he wrote of the risen Saviour —not in Van Buren's proposal to understand him in the

113

unconventional way. The philosopher's viewpoint can hardly be established on empirical grounds either, since there is no conceivable way to settle the claim that the apostle was in fact doing what Van Buren says he was.

Now surely, by Van Buren's own admission concerning the dated character of New Testament language and for other reasons, the Apostle Paul cannot be taken to be using language as either a positivist or an existentialist might use it. He was using it instead as a forthright supernatural theist. If so, how then are we justified in believing that he meant other than what he is ordinarily taken to have meant as a supernatural theist? Moreover, he would have been misled or "bewitched"—to use Wittgenstein's expression again—by his supernatural picture of things *only if he had puzzled about some philosophical problem* such as, for example, the nature of time, as did Saint Augustine in Book X of the *Confessions*. But the apostle was not caught up in any philosophical puzzle. He was using language in his letters to confess Jesus Christ as risen Lord and Saviour.

Van Buren's bewitchment by his positivist picture obliges him to puzzle over whether there really is a God who is "something quite specific"—or, for that matter, whether there is anything supernatural at all. It is he who is not *using* the term "God" as were the New Testament writers. He is puzzling over it and making philosophical proposals concerning it. He is trying to carry out the implications of the positivist picture that holds him captive and that he mistakenly believes to be the only picture that makes sense today. Thus instead of clarifying the matter of the meaning of "God"—which is what the linguistic philosopher is supposed to do—he has only *created* a philosophical puzzle with his proposal to reduce the gospel to its secular meaning.

If the casual reader were to take Van Buren's word for it, he might mistakenly think that Van Buren's method "clarified the meaning of statements by investigating the way in which they are ordinarily used."

And he might be unduly impressed by Van Buren's claim that he arrived at the conclusions of his book after reading Wittgenstein's *Philosophical Investigations*.[15]

The casual reader might also be misled by Van Buren's concluding observations that the difference between his method and Bishop Robinson's is that his "has been characterized by . . . using the tools of linguistic analysis." The reader would be interested also to note that Van Buren rather confidently concludes that had Bishop Robinson "reflected more on the language involved . . . our conclusions would have been even more similar than they are."[16] Although he doesn't do what he set out to do with linguistic philosophy, he does conclude correctly with William Hamilton and Thomas Altizer that a more rigorous methodology might have led Bishop Robinson past his "no-God theism" as Hamilton calls it to the conclusions of the God-is-dead group.

Nothing could be clearer than the fact that any departure from biblical theism is destined to end in outright atheism or—what is even worse—a kind of nontheism whose "god" is something other than or less than the supernatural biblical God in Christ. Either there is really the supernatural biblical God of Abraham, Isaac and Jacob who is the Father of our Lord Jesus Christ or there is a God different from the biblical God or there is no God at all. Since any God that is not the God of the Bible is something less than that God, it would be kind of second-rate good news to discover with the Christian atheists that *this* God is dead. But the good news of the biblical gospel is that the God of biblical hope and promise is very much alive in the person of the risen Christ.

Secular Christianity ennobles neither Christianity nor the worldly life. When it tries to occupy a halfway position like Tillich's or Bultmann's, it fails. Where it

[15] Van Buren, pp. 3, 18n.
[16] *Ibid.*, p. 200.

goes all the way as the radicals have done and as I believe it must, it is no longer Christian. This much the radicals recognized even if they tried to keep the label Christian.

The reach of the secular must be beyond itself to that which grasps and transforms it from beyond. It is not enough to be a man among men. To be fully man is to possess the mind of the living Christ.

Van Buren is deeply devoted to the human figure of Jesus of Nazareth, despite his belief that Jesus has not existed for nearly two thousand years and that the God whom Jesus addressed as Father and to whom He was obedient unto death never existed. How long this devotion will be possible when all the remains of supernatural Christianity have been removed is a matter for interesting speculation.

If Van Buren and the existentialists get their way, Christianity will be finished. But of course they will not get their way, no more than will any of the rest of us. Only the sovereign Lord of Hosts who is Maker of heaven and earth and "has mercy upon whomever he wills, and he hardens the heart of whomever he wills" (Rom. 9:18, RSV) will get His way; and for that we can be profoundly grateful.

9

Postscript Addressed to Christians

ACCORDING TO Carl F. H. Henry, until recently editor
of *Christianity Today,* there are an estimated forty to
forty-five million Evangelicals in English-speaking
North America. The exact figure is not important, but
the magnitude of their widespread witness is important despite their many doctrinal and denominational
differences. An Evangelical, Henry says, is "one who
personally accepts the Gospel as authoritatively stated
in the Bible."[1] Of course this succinct definition could
be interpreted in many ways, and it is obvious that
verbal formulations alone cannot identify the believer.
Yet while it is true that some may be misled by those
who say "This is what I believe too!" or "It isn't what
you believe that makes you a Christian," the fact
remains that whatever may be the *verbal* issue, Evangelicals *do* know who they are and what they stand for
even though they may not always state it clearly or
convincingly or may actually state it very badly. They
do stand together in very distinct ways. Indeed it is
these very ways that often alienate them from those
who are indifferent to them or who find them no longer
relevantly Christian.

The fact is that the Evangelical *is* different. His
love for the Bible and his experience of redemption are
sources of embarrassment for those who do not share

[1] Carl F. H. Henry, editorial in *Christianity Today* (Jan. 5, 1968), p. 25.

117

it. Opposition to Evangelicalism shows itself in many and subtle ways, particularly within the institutional church itself. Christians, it is argued, have been the chief persecutors of nonbelievers and the main instigators of holy wars and intolerance in all of their repugnant forms. No mention is made of the fact that Evangelicals have never understood their duty was to forcibly spread the gospel nor have they claimed that any of the wrongs of those among them were justified. Indeed it is they who have usually deplored the ubiquity of sin and confessed their own with genuine remorse. Nonetheless they get saddled with the sins of *all* Christians including those of the non-Evangelicals themselves. Perhaps the most subtle form of opposition is the claim that what I have just said is paranoid!

There are more Christian believers today than at any other time in history, and believers can be found in almost every community or occupation. Nevertheless their presence irritates many especially within those churches where the "new theology" has captured the allegiance of many if not most of the leadership. Thus the crisis in belief is mainly an internal one, and it is one that far transcends the old liberal-fundamentalist controversy. That controversy had to do mainly with how the Bible was to be understood. The controversy today has to do with whether the Bible has any part at all in the new secularized Christianity.

The chief obstacle to the new secularized Christianity is the old believing one. Believing Christianity holds authoritarian views about God. According to it, God is sovereign, and the Bible is His authority in all matters of belief and practice. He is a heavenly Father. Dependence on Him is not immature or neurotic, nor is it even unsophisticated. Scientists and even some philosophers are evangelical believers.

Believers recognize the underlying fact of the gospel that what might appear to be a meaningless world is in fact a world of joy and promise in Christ. They

118

recognize that the beginning and end of all things is in the hands of the God who revealed Himself in Christ. They recognize that they are new creatures in Christ not through any doing of their own but through the redemptive work of Christ Himself.

The Evangelical does not believe as does Bishop Robinson, for example, that "it is a mark of ... religious immaturity that the 'Father' image inextricably suggests emotional dependence, if not domination."[2] Nor does he agree with Professor Dewart's position in *The Future of Belief* that Christianity has no message, that its mission is to be open to some kind of *presence* in the historic process. Christianity *does* have a message, he believes. It is a message with a mission. Whatever the Great Commission is about, it is not about anything that religion or philosophy or psychotherapy has to offer, nor for that matter, a Gnostic theology. It is about something that the secularist's or existentialist's gospel cannot give. It is about the mighty act of God in Christ on our behalf.

Existentialists can only offer the courage and hope of a man come of age, a man who no longer depends on a caring Father God. Yet if we look to Jesus as the model for our understanding of God, we note that everything He said or did suggested that He believed in a Father God whose care for us is without limit. And when I say this I do not mean that He merely committed Himself to the idea that this might be so or lived *as if* it were so or even that for Him it was a mere figure of speech. I mean that His faith and trust were grounded in the belief that there *was* this kind of God so that even if He did not Himself possess a special supernatural status as the divine Son of God as Evangelicals believe He did, He would still in Hiss *beliefs* nonetheless show us what to believe about God.

The existentialist calls us to an arrogant atheism or a philosophical Christianity. His is not the call of the God of the Bible. Hence it is his self-assertive reinter-

[2] John A. T. Robinson, *The New Reformation?* p. 120.

pretation of the gospel and not the Evangelical's dependent belief that suggests spiritual immaturity.

What then is the trouble with the Evangelical's gospel that leads existentialists to want to reinterpret it or reject it altogether? Is it that it can no longer be understood? I think not. Mark Twain once noted that it was not what he did not understand in the Bible that bothered him. It was what he *did* understand. The trouble with the gospel then is not that it needs to be demythologized, dehellenized or secularized. The trouble is that it is literally *too good to be true*. This is why its acceptance is itself a gift of divine grace even though the believer must open his heart to it. However the believer comes to believe, it is not his task to justify that belief but to share it with others. This I take to be the mandate of the Great Commission.

The Evangelical is a *believer* rather than a *doubter*, a *finder* rather than a *seeker*, a *possessor* rather than a *beggar*. But he is not better off because he is a believer or a finder. He is better off because he possesses the mind of Christ. When he fails to live that mind, he is as the Apostle Paul claimed for himself, the chief of sinners. It is the Christ whose mind he claims that constitutes whatever there is about him that makes him better off. It is not anything about himself. He did not discover Christ by discovering himself. He discovered himself by discovering and *accepting* Christ as Lord of his life. He rejoices in his salvation not because he is seeking it but because he has found it. His praise is easy, spontaneous and genuine. He can pray, and his hope is not secular—not even in the most profound existential sense. His hope is *supernatural* in the full biblical sense. For him, things of the Spirit are distinct from things of the flesh not because there is anything intrinsically bad about the latter but because things of the flesh are not the *final* things.

Bishop Robinson asks: "Is the Church *free* enough to be ... in the midst of all the ambiguities of the 'secular hope' of our day?" This is, he says, "the crucial question for the New Reformation."[3] But the Evangelical must ask: "Is the church willing to *obey* the Great Commission?" *This* is the crucial question. It is not whether the church can effect a workable accommodation. It is whether the church is to obey the God of Jesus and the New Testament or depart into ways of its own making, believing somehow that it can improve upon the faith once delivered to the apostles and the saints.

> Let what you heard from the beginning abide in you. If what you heard from the beginning abides in you, then you will abide in the Son and in the Father.
>
> I John 2:24, RSV

[3] *Ibid.,* p. 104.

Bibliography

Altizer, Thomas J. J., *The Gospel of Christian Atheism*. Philadelphia: Westminster, 1966.

Barth, Karl. *Church Dogmatics, I: The Doctrine of the Word of God*. Edinburgh: T. & T. Clark, 1956.

Baum, Gregory (ed.). *The Future of Belief Debate.* New York: Herder, 1967.

Berger, Peter L. "A Sociological View of the Secularization of Theology," *Journal for the Scientific Study of Religion* (Spring, 1967), p. 5.

Bonhoeffer, Dietrich. *Letters and Papers from Prison*. New York: Macmillan, 1962.

Brunner, H. Emil. *Dogmatics, I: The Christian Doctrine of God*. Philadelphia: Westminster, 1950.

———. *Truth as Encounter*. Philadelphia: Westminster, 1964.

Buber, Martin. *Between Man and Man*. New York: Macmillan, 1965.

———. *The Eclipse of God*. New York: Harper, 1957.

———. *I and Thou*. 2d ed.; New York: Scribner, 1958.

Davies, W. D., and Daube, D. (eds.). *The Background of the New Testament and Its Eschatology*. Cambridge: Cambridge U., 1964.

Dewart, Leslie. *The Future of Belief*. New York: Herder, 1966.

Feuerbach, Ludwig, *Essence of Christianity*. Magnolia, Mass.: Peter Smith, 1958.

Flew, Antony, and Macintyre, A. (eds.). *New Essays in Philosophical Theology*. New York: Macmillan, 1964.

Gill, J. H. "A Case of Mistaken Identity," *The Christian Scholar* (Summer, 1966), p. 149.

Glock, Charles Y., and Stark, Rodney. *Religion and Society in Tension*. New York: Rand McNally, 1965.

Grant, Robert M. *Historical Introduction to the New Testament*. New York: Harper, 1963.

Hall, Robert. "Theology and Analysis," *The Christian Scholar* (Winter, 1965), p. 309.

Heidegger, Martin. *Existence and Being*. Chicago: Regnery, 1949.

Jenkins, David E. *Guide to the Debate About God*. Philadelphia: Westminster, 1966.

Laeuchli, Samuel. *The Language of Faith*. Nashville: Abingdon, 1962.

Macquarrie, John. *The Scope of Demythologizing*. New York: Harper, 1966.

Mascall, Eric L. *The Secularization of Christianity*. New York: Holt, 1966.

Meynell, Hugo A. *Sense, Nonsense, and Christianity*. New York: Sheed & Ward, 1964.

Morris, Leon. *The Abolition of Religion*. Chicago: Inter-Varsity, 1964.

Ogden, Schubert M. *Christ Without Myth*. New York: Harper, 1961.

Pitcher, George (ed.). *Truth*. New York. Prentice-Hall, 1964.

Robinson, John A. T. *Exploration into God*. Palo Alto: Stanford U., 1967.

————. *Honest to God*. Philadelphia: Westminster, 1963.

————. *The New Reformation?* Philadelphia: Westminster, 1965.

Schleiermacher, Friedrich. *On Religion: Speeches to Its Cultured Despisers*. Reprint; New York: Harper, 1958.

Sherwin-White, Adrian N. *Roman Society and Roman Law in the New Testament*. London: Oxford U., 1963.

Tillich, Paul. *Dynamics of Faith*. New York: Harper, 1958.

Van Buren, Paul M. *The Secular Meaning of the Gospel*. New York: Macmillan, 1963.

Index

124